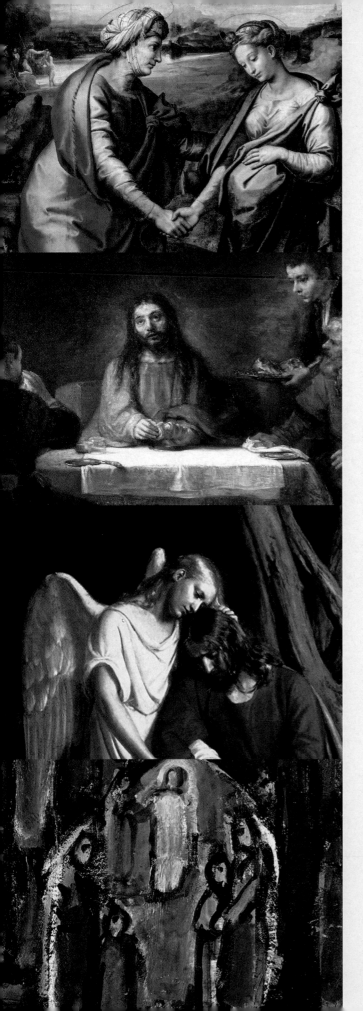

Jesus
&ARCHAEOLOGY

INTRODUCTION

IT IS A FAMILIAR STORY. A baby is born of a virgin and laid in a manger as there is no room in the inn. The baby grows up to be a faith leader who travels through Galilee teaching and performing miracles. As many follow him and turn to his teaching, the authorities of the time become resentful and jealous. In order to maintain the *status quo*, these leaders conspire to have the religious leader eliminated—thus removing their competition. With the aid of the state, the religious leader is crucified, dies and is buried. This is not the end, however. The religious leader transcends death by rising again—as is witnessed by some of his faithful followers—and ascends to heaven confirming his identity as the Son of God.

To this day the birth and death of this baby turned religious luminary is celebrated twice a year, and his life is remembered each week.

This is the story of Jesus.

It reflects traditions that have survived centuries virtually untouched, but can it be enriched by explaining the historical realities of Jesus' birth, world and death?

The quest for the historical Jesus has a multifarious past. But what accounts for this turmoil if the story is so simple? The answer is that the Biblical text does not actually present a simple story. There are contradictions and differences from which questions arise. When one adds the archaeological evidence to these questions, often more questions—rather than answers—appear. This collaborative collection explores some of the more pressing questions by examining both the Biblical text and the archaeological remains.

The place of Jesus' birth is the natural beginning of this journey through history. But it is unclear where Jesus was born.

The traditional answer is Bethlehem, but University of Groningen professor Steve Mason argues that Nazareth—where the New Testament records that Jesus grew up—is a better candidate. Jerome Murphy-O'Connor of the École Biblique et Archéologique in Jerusalem contests Mason and argues in favor of the traditional understanding. The resulting dialogue between these two scholarly luminaries brings the complexity of the issue up close and personal.

Regardless of where Jesus was born, all agree that he "grew and became strong" in Nazareth (Luke 2:39). Ken Dark, the Director of the Research Centre for Late Antiquity and Byzantine Studies at the University of Reading in England, describes the remains of the structure he believes was the boyhood home of Jesus. The house is located under a convent in what was once the first-century village of Nazareth.

Galilee—where Jesus grew up and first began preaching—was under Roman rule. And Jesus was a Jew. So how Jewish was the world in which Jesus was raised and preached? Mark A. Chancey, an Associate Professor at Southern Methodist University in Dallas, explores the questionable place of Judaism in Roman Galilee.

Where is the Pool of Siloam where Jesus healed the blind man (John 9:1–11)? *Biblical Archaeology Review* Editor Hershel Shanks reports on the recent archaeological identification of the impressive first-century pool in Jerusalem where this event is said to have occurred. For centuries tourists and pilgrims have been pointed to the later Byzantine Pool of Siloam that existed not in the first century but in the fourth century C.E.

The collection of works known as the New Testament contains four gospel accounts of the life of Jesus. These gospel accounts relate mostly the teaching and sayings of Jesus. Although they largely agree, at significant points they differ. The matter is further complicated by the numerous apocryphal gospels that also speak of Jesus' life and teaching—but were excluded from the canon. Simon Gathercole, a Reader and Fellow at Cambridge University, explores the noncanonical Gospel of Thomas, a collection of 114 dialogues and sayings attributed to Jesus, for the controversies surrounding the beliefs about inherent evilness of the body and the world in the second-century C.E. Christian community. He also examines the negative view of prayer expressed in this apocryphal gospel and the metaphysical understanding of the Kingdom of God.

Who was responsible for Jesus' death? Helmut Koester, the John H. Morison Research Professor of Divinity and Winn Research Professor of Ecclesiastical History at Harvard Divinity School, takes a close look at the canonical Gospels, Luke in particular, to expose who the evangelists held responsible for Jesus' death. Koester concludes that neither the Pharisees nor the "Jews" in general are blamed—but rather the leadership in Jerusalem and the Roman overlords.

The evening that Jesus spent in Gethsemane is detailed in all three Synoptic Gospels (Matthew 26:36–46; Mark 14:32–42; Luke 22:39–46), but these texts diverge from one another. Jerome Murphy-O'Connor, whom we have met before in this collection, ruminates on these differences and concludes that they could challenge the widely held two-source theory of the Gospels (Mark and Q).

After Jesus was crucified, the Gospels say that he was placed in a tomb that was closed by a rolling stone, but the historicity of this Biblical claim has been questioned by some scholars. Jodi Magness, the Kenan Distinguished Professor for Teaching Excellence in Early Judaism at the University of North Carolina at Chapel Hill, demonstrates that the Biblical telling does indeed fit with the archaeology and practice of the first century C.E., particularly since the tomb was intended for the wealthy Joseph of Arimathea (Mark 15:43–46).

After Jesus' death two disciples encounter Jesus on their way to Emmaus, but they do not recognize him. Later when the three reach Emmaus, the disciples encourage the "stranger" to stay and dine with them. When the "stranger" blesses the bread and gives it to them, the disciples' eyes are opened, and they recognize Jesus (Luke 24:13–53). Where is the mysterious Emmaus? With no less than nine contenders, Hershel Shanks examines archaeologically the options.

In a collection dedicated to asking questions about Jesus in the archaeological record, it is fitting to conclude with an interview of historical Jesus scholar Sean Freyne of Trinity College Dublin. Freyne fields questions from *Biblical Archaeology Review* Editor Hershel Shanks about the Jewish Jesus—both historical and theological. They discuss Jesus' cynical side, the renewal movement that Jesus coopted from John the Baptist, and why Freyne doesn't believe in physical resurrection—and the resurrection he does believe in.

Ellen White
Washington D.C.
February 2016

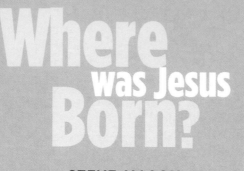

Where was Jesus Born?

STEVE MASON

WHERE WAS JESUS BORN? In Bethlehem, of course, in a manger, because there was no room for Joseph and Mary at the local inn. That's what all the Christmas carols say. And that's what the Gospels say, too.

Or is it?

Once we begin to examine the gospel stories carefully, we find that the answer to this simple question is not so, well, simple. Passages in the Gospels of Matthew and Luke that describe Jesus' birth in Bethlehem have been seamlessly woven together in modern-day Christmas pageants, but the Gospels of Mark and John leave the reader with the distinct impression that Jesus was born not in Bethlehem after all, but in Nazareth.

For the historian, these inconsistencies pose a challenge.[1]

The historian is a time detective, whose task is to raise a specific question about the past, to determine whether there is sufficient evidence to support a probable solution, and finally, to demonstrate how such a solution explains the evidence. Whichever hypothesis most adequately explains the variety of independent evidence becomes a "historical fact"—at least until a better hypothesis comes along.

Applying historical analysis to the earliest Christian writings, most of which are in the New Testament, is not a casual exercise. These are not only the most familiar documents from Western antiquity; they are also revered as scripture by millions of Christians around the globe. Interpreters tend either to overlook ordinary historical questions when reading them or, in some cases, to overcompensate by an unusually aggressive dismissal of

their claims. Nevertheless, if the "history" of Christian origins is to mean anything, we should not simply abandon ourselves to inherited traditions; we should not switch off our normal thought processes when we contemplate Christian beginnings. Instead, we must strive to analyze these texts with the same discipline we use in reconstructing the past behind the narratives of ancient historians such as Livy, Josephus and Tacitus. I realize that some readers consider it inappropriate to apply common historical principles to these texts, and I respect that position. Obviously, I take a different view, which is why I would like to address the question of Jesus' birthplace.[2]

To try to establish where Jesus was born, the historian must examine all the relevant evidence—whether material artifacts, such as coins, pottery and stone inscriptions, or

SHIELDED BY A HAZY MIST, Joseph and Mary escape to Egypt with their newborn son, in an etching by French artist François Millet (1814-1875). According to the Gospel of Matthew, the couple thereby escape King Herod's decree to slaughter all babies born in their hometown, Bethlehem. Matthew is the only Gospel—indeed the only first-century source—to mention Herod's murderous decree and the holy family's subsequent flight. Not even the contemporaneous Jewish historian Josephus, who delighted in unmasking Herod's ferocious nature, speaks of the massacre of the innocents. Further, Matthew's account of the nativity directly contradicts Luke's, which has the family return home to Nazareth immediately after Jesus' birth.

In the accompanying article, Steve Mason asks whether Matthew (or his source) might have invented the story. The question, Mason concludes, must remain open: The inconsistencies and historical improbabilities within the gospel accounts cloud our ability to determine where Jesus was born.

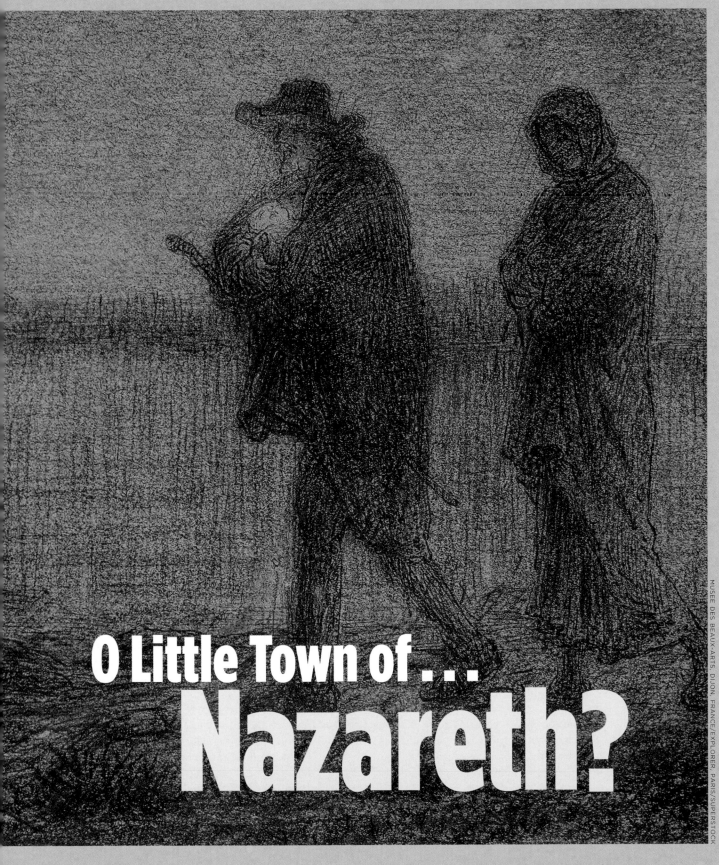

O Little Town of . . . Nazareth?

ancient literature, such as the Gospels, the letters of Paul, the Roman histories and other extrabiblical texts.

In our study of Jesus' birthplace, we can review the archaeological evidence quickly, because there is none: We have no material remains bearing on Jesus' birthplace. The Church of the Nativity in Bethlehem, for example, was not built because of any local memory of Jesus' birth there; it is a much later memorial, constructed on the site of a fourth-century church erected by the emperor Constantine when Christianity received state recognition. Constantine probably selected the spot based on the then-famous stories recorded in the Gospels of Matthew and Luke.

That leaves us with the texts.

Not one of the first- and early-second-century A.D. non-Christian authors who mention Christians in passing—the Jewish historian Flavius Josephus, the Romans Tacitus and Pliny—provides us with any helpful information about Jesus' birthplace. We have only the earliest Christian texts, written by the first three generations of Jesus' followers, from the time of Jesus' death in about 30 A.D. to roughly 150 A.D. These writings—and only these writings—are the sources we must examine.

The only texts that are dated with some confidence to the first Christian generation (about 30 to 65 A.D.) are the New Testament letters genuinely attributed to Paul. From the second generation, we have the four canonical Gospels. The Gospels are generally dated to between 65 and 100 A.D., with Mark being the earliest and Matthew and Luke dating to the end of that period. John may fall almost anywhere within this range.[3]

But what did these writers really know about Jesus' birthplace? And what motivated them to speak of Jesus' birth at all?

Let's begin with our earliest source, Paul.

In all of the letters that we have, Paul never mentions any geographical location in connection with Jesus.

This absence can be explained in several ways: Such references may have been irrelevant to his purposes; or he may have assumed that his (converted) readers already knew of these traditions and therefore that he didn't need to mention them; or he may not have known much about the geography of Jesus' life. Admittedly, much can be attributed to the first category

(irrelevance), since Paul was primarily concerned with Jesus' status between his crucifixion and his return from heaven, and not so much with the mundane details of Jesus' life. When he referred to Jesus' betrayal and described the Last Supper (1 Corinthians 11:23), for example, he almost certainly knew that these events took place near Jerusalem, but he had no reason to bring it up.

Did Paul know any tradition about the place of Jesus' birth? Since he does not mention one, we cannot be certain. But there is another way to approach this question, which is to ask whether it would have helped Paul's arguments—or those of his correspondents—to mention Jesus' birthplace if he did know about it.

Paul wrote letters, not essays, and he was in frequent debate with other Christians whose views differed from his own. His letters preserve not only his own perspectives, therefore, but also traces of his correspondents'. For example, many of Paul's gentile converts were attracted by Judaism; some of the males were even willing to undergo circumcision (Galatians 4:21, 5:2-12). So Paul discussed circumcision at several points, even though he probably would not have raised the subject if he were simply presenting his own views. So, we can ask not only whether Jesus' birthplace was an issue for Paul, but whether his letters indicate that it was an issue for any first-generation Christians.

Paul mentions Jesus' ancestry only twice, and then incidentally. The first time, he is writing to some gentile converts in Galatia, trying to discourage them from their zeal to adopt Judaism. Just as Jesus, though he had been born "under the law" and "of a woman," achieved spiritual sonship and freedom from the law (Galatians 4:4), so also the Galatians, who have achieved spiritual sonship, must not regress by enslaving themselves to a physical regimen (as Paul characterizes the Jewish calendar and circumcision).

The second time Paul mentions Jesus' birth, he is addressing converts in Rome. In this context, he concedes to his readers Jesus' physical ancestry from David, but he highlights Jesus' designation as "Son of God" for all humanity (Romans 1:4).

Scholars differ significantly in their understanding of Paul's motives,* but I would argue that even if he had known of the Bethlehem tradition,

*See, for example, John G. Gager, "Paul's Contradictions: Can They Be Resolved?" *Bible Review*, December 1998, and the response by Ben Witherington, "Laying Down the Law," *Bible Review*, April 1999.

JESUS EMERGES FROM NAZARETH a grown man in Georges Rouault's 1948 oil painting, just as in the Gospel of Mark, which makes no mention of Jesus' birth in Bethlehem or of his childhood. Mark consistently refers to Jesus as "Jesus of Nazareth." The evangelist's motivation is difficult to determine: Did Mark simply not know of the Bethlehem tradition, or did he wish to conceal the story in order to distance Jesus from Jewish traditions of a Messiah from Bethlehem, the home of King David?

it would not have served his interests to mention it. Among his gentile converts, attraction to Judaism was an ongoing phenomenon. Paul's consistent line was to draw them back to the "new creation" that he believed had supplanted Judaism (2 Corinthians 5:17; Galatians 6:15). A birth in Bethlehem, King David's home, would naturally cement Jesus' Jewish-messianic affiliation,[4] which Paul was trying to move beyond. Thus it is not surprising that Paul might not have mentioned Jesus' birth in Bethlehem even if he knew about it, for mentioning Bethlehem would only have given fuel to his Jewish Christian opponents. First, in Romans 1:3, Paul does concede Jesus' Davidic descent: Although he was son of David "according to the flesh" (a negative category for Paul), he became son of God (much grander,

no?) by his resurrection from the dead—from the physical to the spiritual. Second, although someone else might argue that Davidic ancestry would increase Jesus' appeal for Paul and his readers, I cannot see that. Paul is in a dire struggle with the Jewish Christians precisely because he has been preaching to gentiles a dying and rising savior—Jesus denuded of Jewish connections. It would only help his opponents to emphasize Jesus' Davidic ancestry. For Paul, that is more or less irrelevant: Jesus is the son of God, for all nations alike, without any special Jewish connection. Judaism has, for Paul, ended.

More telling, perhaps, is that Paul's correspondents did not seize upon Jesus' birth in Bethlehem, if they had known about it, as evidence of the Jewish nature of Jesus. From Paul's letters, we know that his correspondents quoted copiously from Jewish scripture (including the terms of the covenant with Abraham and Moses) and that they appealed to the examples of Jesus' own brothers and students, who no doubt spoke of Jesus' Jewish practices (2 Corinthians 11:5-29; Galatians 1:6-11, 2:11-21, 3:6-21). They marshaled arguments for Jesus' Jewish context, and Paul was forced to reply to them in some detail. But as far as we can tell, the circumstances of Jesus' birth never came up. If Jesus was known to have had a miraculous birth in the auspicious village of Bethlehem, wouldn't someone in this first generation have made some sort of appeal

"FEAR NOT," an angel reassures the sleeping Joseph, carved in ivory on this late-11th-century plaque from southern Italy, now in the Victoria & Albert Museum. Three times in the Gospel of Matthew an angel appears to Joseph—instructing him to take Mary as his wife, warning him to flee to Egypt with his family and finally telling him when it is safe to return to Israel (Matthew 1:20-23, 13-15, 19-20). Quoting scripture, the angel reassures Joseph that each of these actions "fulfills what was spoken through the prophet." The marriage and subsequent birth, the angel insists, fulfill Isaiah 7:14: "Look, the virgin shall conceive and bear a son." The sojourn in Egypt fulfills Hosea 11:1: "Out of Egypt I have called my son."

Matthew's proclivity for presenting Jesus' birth as the realization of ancient prophecy leads author Mason to ask whether the gospel writer might have reworked the details of the birth story in order to better match Old Testament predictions.

to it? Yet, in the end, we are left with complete silence about Jesus' birthplace from the time of Jesus' death to about 65 A.D.

The Gospels are at least a generation removed from Jesus' birth. It is extremely unlikely that any of these authors was an eyewitness to Jesus' life. They all relied on oral and written sources. Indeed, the author of Luke freely admits at the outset that the events he describes "were handed on to us by those who from the beginning were eyewitnesses" (Luke 1:2). The Fourth Gospel concludes with a similar disclosure (John 21:24).[5] Further, all four Gospels are anonymous texts. The familiar attributions of the Gospels to Matthew, Mark, Luke and John come from the mid-second century and later, and we have no good historical reason to accept these attributions.

Although we cannot identify the authors or the precise dates of the Gospels, we can say something about the literary relationship of the first three Gospels (the Synoptic Gospels).[6] The dominant hypothesis today is that Mark served as a source for both Matthew and Luke and that the extensive material common to Matthew and Luke but not paralleled in Mark comes from another shared source (called Q for convenience), which is now lost.* I make no use of Q here, though I do assume for argument's sake that Matthew and Luke used Mark as a source.[7]

Did the author of Mark, the earliest of the four Gospels, know anything about the place of Jesus' birth?

Unlike Luke and Matthew, which include the familiar birth stories, Mark opens with Jesus as an adult, who simply emerges from Nazareth: "In those days, Jesus came from Nazareth of Galilee and was baptized by John in the Jordan" (Mark 1:9). When Jesus moves to Capernaum, everyone continues to address him as a Nazarene. "What have you to do with us, Jesus of Nazareth?" ask the locals in the Capernaum synagogue (Mark 1:24; see also 10:47, 14:67, 16:6). When Jesus returns to his "hometown" (Greek *patris*, "ancestral home"), he goes to Nazareth (Mark 6:1). When he teaches in the Nazareth synagogue, the locals are offended at his pretensions because they have long known him, his mother, his brothers and his sisters (Mark 6:1-3). Although the author does not say "since birth," that seems to be assumed. Jesus

*On the hypothesized Gospel of Q, see Stephen J. Patterson, "Q—The Lost Gospel," *Bible Review,* October 1993, and "Yes, Virginia, There Is a Q," *Bible Review,* October 1995.

Bethlehem in the Bible

If the gospel writers were drawing on Old Testament references to Bethlehem to bolster Jesus' identification as the Messiah, they certainly had plenty of passages to choose from. Bethlehem (the name means "House of Bread") appears almost 50 times in more than ten books of the Hebrew Bible.

The city, just 5 miles south of Jerusalem, is first mentioned in conjunction with the death of the matriarch Rachel. "So Rachel died, and she was buried on the way to Ephrath (that is, Bethlehem)" (Genesis 35:19, 48:7).*

More important to our story, Bethlehem is also where Ruth and Boaz meet, marry and bear their son Obed, the father of Jesse, the father of King David. God sends the prophet Samuel to Bethlehem to find the new king, saying, "I will send you to Jesse the Bethlehemite, for I have provided myself

*Some scholars claim that the parenthetical phrase "that is, Bethlehem" is a later gloss, and that Rachel is buried in Benjamin, near Ramah, as described in 1 Samuel 10:2.

a king among his sons" (1 Samuel 16:1). Bethlehem remained a city of significance throughout the stories of David's life and reign; while fighting the Philistines, who had a garrison at Bethlehem, David requests water from the well of Bethlehem (2 Samuel 23:15).

And there's more. The Book of Micah, written around the time of the Assyrian siege of Samaria in the late eighth century B.C., looks forward to a new day when Israel will be led by a ruler from Bethlehem (perhaps a ruler "from David's line"):

But you Bethlehem of Ephrathah, the least of the clans of Judah, from you will come for me a future ruler of Israel whose origins go back to the distant past, to the days of old.

Hence Yahweh will abandon them only until she who is in labor gives birth, and then those who survive of his race will be reunited to the Israelites.

He will take his stand and he will shepherd them with the power of

Yahweh, with the majesty of the name of his God, and they will be secure, for his greatness will extend henceforth to the most distant parts of the country.

He himself will be peace!

MICAH 5:1-4

It is this prophecy of Micah that will be quoted by Matthew as evidence of Jesus' messiahship.

The next (and last) references to Bethlehem in the Hebrew Bible record how many of the city's residents returned from the Babylonian Exile: 123, according to Ezra 2:21 (see also Nehemiah 7:26).

Following the birth narratives in the Gospels, Bethlehem is never again mentioned in the New Testament. Thenceforth Jesus is known as Jesus of Nazareth, and it is this town, 15 miles west of the Sea of Galilee, that becomes a fixture of the New Testament. Unlike Bethlehem, Nazareth is not mentioned once in the Old Testament; the village was not occupied until the second or first century B.C.

responds famously: "Prophets are not without honor, except in their hometown, among their own kin, and in their own home" (Mark 6:4).

The author of Mark is not simply silent about Bethlehem; he appears to assume that Jesus was born and raised in Nazareth. Anyone who read Mark alone, without benefit of Matthew or Luke (which Mark's first readers would not have known), would receive that impression. Mark makes no effort to explain any other origin.

But does this mean that Mark knows nothing of a Bethlehem birth? Or might Mark, like Paul, have had strong motives to deny any connection between Jesus and that town?

Mark's story is very much in the tradition of Paul's: The Gospel portrays Jesus as the dying and rising savior, who will return shortly to save his followers, represented by all nations. In Mark, Jesus is fundamentally, indeed fatally, alienated from Judaism. "What is this? A new teaching!" his Jewish listeners gasp (Mark 1:27). Jesus' Jewish family, students and hometown folk are major disappointments to him because they

do not understand him. Later in Mark, it is the Pharisees (members of a Jewish sect) who will conspire with Herod to murder Jesus (Mark 3:6). Even if the author of Mark had known about a Bethlehem birth, he, like Paul, may have had reason to suppress that information in order to disassociate Jesus from Jewish categories.

In keeping with this dislocation from Judaism, Mark's Jesus directly challenges the notion that the Messiah should be a descendant of David: "While Jesus was teaching in the Temple, he said, 'How can the scribes say that the Messiah is the son of David? ... David himself calls him Lord; so how can he be his [David's] son?'" (Mark 12:35-37). If Davidic descent itself is unimportant in Mark, birth in David's hometown is irrelevant.

On the other hand, at least one passage in Mark indicates that the author, rather than trying to hide the traditions surrounding Jesus' birth, truly did not know about them: Once, when Jesus returns home and a crowd gathers around him, his family and friends go out to seize him, thinking that he is "out of his mind" because of his behavior (Mark 3:21). If the author of Mark (or his Christian readers) had known about the heavenly revelations to Mary and Joseph, about the shepherds and the Magi, and about the great celebration at the time of Jesus' birth in Bethlehem, would he not have mentioned this?

Although both Matthew and Luke appear to have drawn on Mark, these later Gospels often disagree significantly with their source. The authors of Matthew and Luke were especially concerned with re-establishing Jesus within Judaism to some degree. And the story that they had heard about Jesus' birth in Bethlehem helped them do so.

Matthew's intentions are clear from his opening lines, which firmly establish Jesus' Jewish roots: "An account of the genealogy of Jesus the Messiah, the son of David, the son of Abraham." Matthew goes on to list the generations from Abraham to Jesus—including 14 from Abraham to David, 14 from David to the Exile and a final 14 from the Exile to Jesus. Only then does Matthew describe the birth: "Now the birth of Jesus the Messiah took place in this way. When his mother Mary had been engaged to Joseph, but before they lived together, she was found to be with child from the Holy Spirit" (Matthew 1:18). An angel encourages Joseph not to abandon Mary:

"Joseph, son of David, do not be afraid to take Mary as your wife, for the child conceived in her is from the Holy Spirit. She will bear a son, and you are to name him Jesus, for he will save his people from their sins." All this took place to fulfill what had been spoken by the Lord through the prophet [quoting Isaiah 7:14*]: "Look, the virgin shall conceive and bear a son, and they shall name him Emmanuel," which means "God is with us." When Joseph awoke from sleep, he did as the angel of the Lord commanded him; he took her as his wife, but had no marital relations with her until she had borne a son; and he named him Jesus. (Matthew 1:20-25)

Only then are we given the time and location of the birth: "In the time of King Herod, after Jesus was born in Bethlehem of Judea, wise men from the East came to Jerusalem, asking, 'Where is the child who has been born king of the Jews?'" Frightened, Herod calls together his chief priests and scribes and asks them where the

*See J. Edward Barrett, "Can Scholars Take the Virgin Birth Seriously?" *Bible Review,* October 1988.

When Was Jesus Born?

Not only is there a problem determining where Jesus was born—pinpointing when he was born presents a challenge, too. Despite all the festivities celebrating New Year's 2000 as the 2,000th year since Jesus' birth, most scholars are certain that he was not born in that hazy period between 1 B.C. and 1 A.D. (remember, there is no year 0). In fact, he was probably born several years before then—a seeming paradox if ever there was one! But remember that "Before Christ" was a term established several centuries after Jesus.

The current dating system, which places January 1, 1 A.D., a week after Jesus' birth, was established in about 525 A.D. by Dionysius Exiguus (Dennis the Little), a Scythian monk, who hoped to repair a division in the church over the dates of Easter by preparing a new calendar. Rather than use the then-standard Diocletian system (counting the years since the reign of this late-third-century emperor, who had persecuted the Christians), Dionysius decided to count from Jesus' birth. To do this, he used an earlier calendric system, which dated to many centuries before Jesus' time—a Roman system based on the establishment of Rome. He fixed Jesus' birth date as December 25, 753 A.U.C. (*Ab Urbe Condita,* from the founding of the city of Rome). It is not known how Dionysius chose that date. One theory is that he based it on the Book of Luke, which states that "Jesus was about thirty years old when he began his work" (Luke 3:23) and that this occurred "in the fifteenth year of the reign of Emperor Tiberius" (Luke 3:1). Tiberius's reign began around 767 A.U.C., or 14 A.D., so 754 A.U.C. became 1 A.D. Dionysius's system of counting years gradually caught on: Charlemagne made it nearly universal in the ninth century, and the calendar we use today maintains Dionysius's calculations, with a few adjustments made by Pope Gregory in 1582. (Why December 25th was accepted as Jesus' birthday is even more obscure; it may be related to the Roman festival of Saturnalia, which was celebrated on that date. It may also be related to the Jewish tradition of performing circumcisions one week after a birth—in Jesus' case, on January 1.)

But Dionysius had miscalculated. As Matthew's Gospel tells us, Jesus was born during the reign of Herod the Great. Herod died in 4 B.C., as is known from outside sources, such as Josephus, and from the dates of contemporaneous Roman leaders. This means that Jesus must have been born before 4 B.C. Various calculations, based on astronomy, history and the Bible, have come up with dates between 7 and 4 B.C. But that won't change anyone's plans, or their calendars.

Messiah was to be born. Quoting the prophet Micah (see box, p. 9), they reply: "In Bethlehem of Judea; for so it has been written by the prophet: 'And you, Bethlehem, in the land of Judah, are by no means least among the rulers of Judah; for from you shall come a ruler who is to shepherd my people Israel'" (Matthew 2:5-6).

In Matthew's account, Jesus' parents initially live in Bethlehem, just south of Jerusalem (Matthew 2:1,11). It is only when a paranoid King Herod massacres the newborns in that region (Matthew 2:16) that the family flees to Egypt. Although the new parents wish to return home to Bethlehem in Judea after Herod's death, they receive divine instruction to settle in "a town called Nazareth" (Matthew 2:23), which is introduced at the end of Matthew's birth narrative. Each of the family's movements, the author repeatedly points out, "fulfills what was spoken through the prophet" (Matthew 1:22, 2:5,15,17,23), quoting Isaiah, Micah and perhaps other prophets. Clearly, Matthew wants to show that Jesus stood in continuity with his Jewish past.

Matthew's allusions to Micah and other prophets raise a crucial question: Is it more likely that the author included a Bethlehem birth for Jesus because he knew that this had in fact happened or because he knew of the passages in scripture and thought it important to describe Jesus' career in the language of the prophets? This may seem cynical, but it is an unavoidable issue for the historian. Later in Matthew, we find the author clearly adjusting the story of Jesus' life to match the Old Testament record. For example, in Mark, when Jesus enters Jerusalem, he rides on a donkey colt (Mark 11:2). The author of Matthew parallels Mark's story almost verbatim, except that he has Jesus riding on both a donkey and its colt (Matthew 21:2,7). The author explains that this action fulfills Zechariah 9:9, according to which the king of Israel should come riding on a donkey and a colt (Matthew 21:4-5).**

Has the author of Matthew similarly manipulated the birth account?

**The author of Matthew misunderstood the rhetorical device called *hendiadys*, often used in Hebrew poetry, in which a term is repeated and preceded with the particle, often translated "and." The second mention of the term actually modifies the first. See Harvey Minkoff, "Searching for the Better Text," *Bible Review,* August 1999. For another example of Matthew accommodating the story to scripture, see the case of Judas's death (Matthew 26:15, 27:3-10), which is presented as fulfilling a scripture citation in wording but does not agree with Luke's account (Acts 1:16-20).

Matthew's infancy narrative can be suspiciously formulaic, beginning with the neat division of Jesus' genealogy into three sets of 14 generations, which do not accord with the Old Testament parallels or even with the text of Matthew itself.[8] Such patterns suggest that the author is not simply reporting on events.[9]

Further, despite Matthew's efforts to construct neat literary patterns, the Bethlehem story is not well incorporated into the rest of the text. Immediately following the birth narrative, Matthew appears to revert to Mark's version of events. In chapters 3 to 28 of Matthew, which paraphrase Mark extensively, Jesus speaks of Nazareth as his ancestral home or birthplace (Matthew 13:57) and Jesus is said to be "from Nazareth" (Matthew 21:11, 26:71). Joseph, a central figure in the birth narrative, disappears entirely (in keeping with Mark, which never mentions Joseph), and the birth story is nowhere recalled in later chapters of Matthew. Curiously, Matthew even preserves Jesus' challenge to the Messiah's descent from David (Matthew 22:41-45).

Finally, there are obvious historical difficulties with Matthew's birth narrative, including the mysterious star that somehow identified a particular house in Bethlehem (Matthew 2:9-11) and Herod's slaughter of children—an event that is not recorded in any other first-century A.D. source. Matthew's contemporary Josephus wrote several volumes excoriating Herod for his violations of Jewish custom.[10] It seems highly unlikely that if a slaughter of babies had taken place near Jerusalem, Josephus would not have heard about it and used it as an example of Herod's heinous crimes.

The most serious doubts about the historicity of Matthew's Bethlehem story, however, come to light as we compare his text with Luke's.

Luke's Bethlehem story is not complementary to Matthew's, filling in the gaps, as is often assumed. Rather, it is an irreconcilably different account from beginning to end: in story line, supporting characters, geographical and historical detail, and style. Both accounts explain that Jesus was born to the Virgin Mary and Joseph in Bethlehem and grew up in Nazareth, but that is all they share.

The Gospel of Luke opens with two birth narratives—John the Baptist's and Jesus'—claiming that the two men were relatives (Luke 1:5-2:21, esp. 1:36-45). We first read of how John's elderly parents, late in life, will give birth to a son; then we read of the annunciation to Mary. Next we're told the circumstances of the birth and infancy of John and then of Jesus.

Luke's account of Jesus' birth opens with Mary and Joseph living in Nazareth (not Bethlehem, as Matthew has it). Near the end of Mary's pregnancy, during the rule of the emperor Augustus and the Syrian governor Quirinius, the couple must travel to Bethlehem for a worldwide census (never mentioned in Matthew), which requires people to return to their ancestral homes (Luke 2:1-5). Joseph goes to Bethlehem because he belongs to the "house and ancestry" (*oikos kai patria*) of King David, who lived a millennium earlier. Jesus is born just after his parents arrive in Bethlehem. There is no room for them at the inn, so he is born in the local manger (Luke 2:7), where he is adored by the local shepherds. Once Mary's 33 days of purification are over (Luke 2:22; cf. Leviticus 12:4), she presents Jesus in the Temple with an appropriate sacrifice; then she and Joseph return home to Nazareth (Luke 2:39; in Matthew, they only settle in Nazareth after traveling to Egypt).

The author of Luke, like the author of Matthew, wishes to establish Jesus within Judaism.[11] Does he mention Bethlehem simply to strengthen his argument?[12]

Just as Matthew's account presents historical problems, so does Luke's. The census, mentioned only by Luke, provides the historical context for Luke's birth narrative. We do have outside corroboration of a census of the Jews under the Syrian governor Quirinius, when Judea was directly annexed to Rome as a province: This census plays a significant role in the histories of Josephus because it reportedly sparked a popular revolt.[13]

Luke's effort to link Jesus' birth in Bethlehem with the census is, however, plagued by historical inconsistencies and improbabilities.[14] The census described by Josephus occurred in 6 A.D., several years after Jesus' birth (see box, p. 10). It was not a worldwide census, although it apparently included Syria along with Judea. And requiring people to travel far away from where they were living would defeat the purpose of a Roman census, which was to assess *current* property for taxation. Moreover, only the household head would need to report to a

"AND SHE BROUGHT FORTH her firstborn son, and laid him in a manger." So wrote Luke in his remarkable birth story, set here in a fanciful Italianate landscape. Commissioned to hang in the Church of the Holy Trinity in Florence, "The Adoration of the Shepherds" (1485) by Domenico Ghirlandaio includes the manger where Mary and Joseph were forced to spend the night because there was "no room at the inn" (Luke 2:7). On a distant hill, an angel announces the miraculous birth to the shepherds "keeping watch over their flock by night" (Luke 2:8-14). In the foreground, these shepherds, their skin tanned by years in the fields, marvel at the newborn child (2:16-18) while the gray-haired Joseph casts his eyes toward heaven. In Ghirlandaio's rendition, Roman ruins with a straw roof serve as the makeshift manger; behind the babe lies a gaping sarcophagus—a reminder of his impending death and resurrection.

According to Luke, the birth took place suddenly when Joseph and Mary were traveling from their home in Nazareth to Bethlehem for an imperial census. But there's a glitch in Luke's account: The only comparable historical census took place in 6 A.D., several years after Jesus' birth.

local administrative center. Finally, it would be absurd to require all the thousands of descendants of David, who had lived a thousand years earlier, to return to his birthplace. David himself moved to Jerusalem after conquering the city, and so a descendant of David would also be a descendant of many others—from Jerusalem.

These are not the only problems with Luke's narrative: Following the initial account of Jesus' birth in Luke, the remarkable Bethlehem story plays no further role (just as in Matthew). Significantly, the author describes Nazareth as "the place where Jesus *was raised*" (Luke 4:16) rather than as Jesus' native town (cf. Mark 6:1), but Jesus continues to be identified as "Jesus of Nazareth" or "the Nazarene" (Luke 4:34, 18:37, 24:19; Acts 2:22, 3:6, 4:10, 6:14 et al.). Further, when Jesus comes to trial, Luke—alone—insists that because he was a Galilean by origin, Jesus had to be tried by Herod Antipas, the tetrarch of Galilee who was visiting Jerusalem for Passover (Luke 23:6-7). There is no remembrance of Bethlehem as Jesus' ancestral home.[15]

The Gospel of John offers no account of Jesus' birth, but the text nevertheless reveals many early Christian assumptions regarding Jesus' birthplace.

Most tellingly, in John 7:40-44 a crowd is debating whether Jesus is a prophet or the Messiah; some of the people object, saying: "The Messiah does not come from Galilee, does he? Didn't the scripture say that the Messiah comes from the seed of David, from Bethlehem—the village where David was from?" No one says, "Wait a minute. Jesus was indeed born in Bethlehem!" The author of John does not seem to know that Jesus was born in Bethlehem.

Similarly, when the disciple Nathanael is told that Jesus is the one described in the Law and Prophets and comes "from Nazareth," Nathanael retorts, "Can anything good come from Nazareth?" (John 1:45-46).

The contrast between what Jesus appears to be (human) and what he really is (divine) is a theme found throughout the Gospel: Similarly, Jesus *appears* to die miserably, as any man would, when hoisted on the cross, whereas in reality the cross marks his exaltation and the completion of his mission (John 12:32, 19:30). It fits with John's entire approach, therefore, to use Jesus' humble birth in Nazareth as a counterpoint to his heavenly origin.

Let us return to our "simple" question: Where was Jesus born? Does any hypothesis concerning Jesus' birthplace explain the evidence?

If Jesus was born in Bethlehem and this was widely known among his followers, then Jesus' distinguished place of birth must have been regarded as irrelevant to any early Christian discussion that has left traces in Paul's letters. This would be surprising, though not entirely improbable.

Similarly, the author of Mark might have suppressed this information, while at the same time implying that Jesus was from Nazareth, out of a desire to separate Jesus from Jewish traditions.

The author of John, too, may have concealed the Bethlehem tradition; this, however, is more difficult to explain, because if it was widely known that Jesus was from Bethlehem, that knowledge would have undercut the author's use of irony based on Jesus' ignominious origins as a Galilean and, more specifically, a Nazarene.

Even harder to explain are the extensive disagreements and numerous historical improbabilities in the only two texts that posit a Bethlehem birth: Matthew and Luke. Neither narrative indicates that its author knew the circumstances of Jesus' birth.

Finally, if Jesus' birth in Davidic Bethlehem was widely known among early Christians, why didn't this knowledge have a greater effect on the thinking of the first four generations of Christians, who were most exercised to prove Jesus' messiahship to doubting Jews?

If the Bethlehem hypothesis does not explain the evidence very well, would another site, such as Nazareth, work better? Perhaps, but our survey of the evidence suggests that early Christians simply did not know much about Jesus' birth. This is only to be expected, since Jesus' main significance for many of his earliest followers had to do with his teaching, death, resurrection and expected return. When Jesus began his ministry as an adult, he was known to his followers as "Jesus of Nazareth"—a title that persists in all the second-generation texts. Christians throughout the first generation reasonably assumed, as did the later authors of Mark and John, that Jesus was born and raised in Nazareth. It was fairly late when some Christians first became more interested in the question, and this accords with a demonstrable tendency in later Christian history to cultivate information about Jesus' birth and early years. Even by the time of Matthew and Luke, reliable information about Jesus' birth was no longer available. These authors took the basic proposition (probably from an earlier, now-lost source) that Jesus, the son of David, had been born in Bethlehem before Joseph and Mary had become intimate. This proposition could easily have originated in reflection upon Micah 5:2 and developed from there. That would explain why their stories fit their respective literary proclivities so well. It was only in the mid-second century, after their accounts were in wide circulation, that Jesus' birth in Bethlehem, the city of David, would capture the Christian imagination. Only then did the Bethlehem birth become a significant argument for Jesus' messiahship and the evolving doctrine of the incarnation—of God becoming man.

Where was Jesus born? Was it Bethlehem or Nazareth or even Sepphoris, Tiberias or Jerusalem? We cannot know for sure because the early Christians themselves apparently did not know. ▨

[1] I do not claim that the arguments presented here are original. The editors have invited me to make a summary statement on the issue.

[2] In the ancient Mediterranean, one's ancestry was public business. Membership in the aristocracy was a condition of success in many spheres. City or town of origin was considered important, even if one had long since moved from

the family home and birthplace. Unprecedented numbers of people traveled on the long Roman roads and relatively safe Roman seas; nevertheless, those from the eastern Mediterranean, who lacked the traditional three Roman names, were usually known as "*X of Y*," where *Y* was the ancestral home (Greek, *patris* or *oikos*)—Justus of Tiberias, Ptolemy of Ascalon, Nicolas of Damascus and so on. Even villages could be important for identifying someone. In discussing events in Galilee, Josephus distinguishes those whose ancestry was in a particular town from those who were merely living there but had their family heritage elsewhere (Josephus, *Life* 16.126,142,162). For everyday purposes, Judea and Galilee were much like other Mediterranean locales in this respect.

[3] My assumptions about the authorship and dating of these texts are generally accepted in New Testament scholarship and are presented as standard views in universities, seminaries and many Bible colleges. A detailed and balanced account may be found in E.P. Sanders and Margaret Davies, *Studying the Synoptic Gospels* (Philadelphia: Trinity Press International, 1990). See also Steve Mason and Tom Robinson, eds., *An Early Christian Reader* (Peabody, MA: Hendrickson, 2001).

[4] Several prophetic texts had promised a restoration of King David's ancient throne, which had been lost at the time of the Babylonian destruction in 586 B.C. In the Book of Samuel, the Lord sends David the following message: "When your days are fulfilled and you lie down with your ancestors, I will raise up your offspring after you, who shall come forth from your body, and I will establish his kingdom ... I will be a father to him, and he shall be a son to me ... Your house and your kingdom shall be made sure forever before me; your throne shall be established forever" (2 Samuel 7:12-16); see also Isaiah 9:7. For the hopes for David's royal descendant Zerubbabel after the Exile, see Haggai 2:20-23; Zechariah 4:6-10; see also Sirach 49:11; 1 Maccabees 2:57; 2 Esdras 12:32; Psalms of Solomon 17; and frequent me ntions in rabbinic literature. Although it is doubtful that physical descent from David could be confidently traced a thousand years after he had died, establishing some kind of connection with David might have been critical for a messianic figure or other leader in Jesus' time. According to the fourth-century church historian Eusebius, the emperor Domitian (81-96 A.D.) launched a campaign against descendants of David because he was afraid of the competition (Eusebius, *Church History* 3.19-20). The story itself is unlikely, but it highlights the importance of Davidic lineage in Christian thinking at least. And when Rabbi Akiva allegedly endorsed Simeon bar-Kokhba, leader of the Second Jewish Revolt against Rome (132-135 A.D.), as the Messiah, one of his colleagues is said to have demurred on the ground that this man was not a descendant of David (Jerusalem Talmud, *Ta'anit* 4.5 [68d]). See Ephraim Urbach, *The Sages: Their Concepts and Beliefs*, trans. Israel Abrahams (Cambridge, MA: Harvard Univ. Press, 1979), p. 674. In later periods, both the Jewish patriarchs and the heads of the Babylonian Jewish communities would be furnished with suitable Davidic ancestries (*Genesis Rabbah* 33). See, conveniently, Isaiah Gafni, "The World of the Talmud," in Hershel Shanks, ed., *Christianity and Rabbinic Judaism: A Parallel History of Their Origins and Early Development* (Washington, DC: Biblical Archaeology Society, 1992), pp. 229, 248, 263. The medieval *Seder Olam Zutta* traced a Davidic lineage for the Babylonian exilarch. So lineage in general was important, and many considered Davidic lineage essential for messianic figures. The Dead Sea Scrolls and other texts indicate that some groups hoped for priestly and/or prophetic anointed figures (messiahs). So, too, the Talmud reflects a variety of messianic hopes, even though the dominant language speaks of the "Son of David." See

Jacob Neusner, *Messiah in Context: Israel's History and Destiny in Formative Judaism* (Philadelphia: Fortress, 1984).

[5] Further, for the Synoptics, the extensive literary borrowing, the thematic arrangement of discrete episodes (e.g., conflict stories, teaching examples) with only the loosest chronological links, and the free adjustment of this material for literary purposes indicate that the authors—like other ancient biographers—are weaving material relayed to them by tradition rather than simply reporting what they saw.

[6] The term synoptic, from Greek for "seeing together," refers to the fact that when the Gospels of Matthew, Mark and Luke are printed side by side in three parallel columns, their numerous correspondences can be "seen together" at a glance.

[7] My basic point would remain intact, however, even if it turned out that the texts had some other relationship.

[8] In Matthew 1:2-17, the numbers of generations in each block are actually 13, 14, 13 instead of the three 14-generation blocks claimed by the author.

[9] On the various patterns, see Raymond E. Brown, *The Birth of the Messiah* (Garden City, NY: Doubleday, 1977), pp. 48-54, 96-121. The powerful Matthean literary themes of scriptural continuity and the coming of foreigners into salvation (the Magi; cf. Matthew 8:11-13, 28:16-20) can hardly be missed.

[10] Josephus, *Antiquities of the Jews* 14-17.

[11] Whereas Matthew locates Jesus' gradual rejection by Israel near the middle of the story (Matthew 11-12), Luke delays this until the very end of Jesus' life, when he encounters the Temple authorities in Jerusalem (Luke 19:47); and it is only in the second volume, which we know as Acts, after the proclamation of Jesus' resurrection, that Israel in general rejects him. Throughout Luke and the early chapters of Acts, Jesus and his followers remain steadfastly committed to the laws of Moses, and they get along fairly well with Pharisees and common people (see Luke 7:36, 11:37, 13:31, 14:1, 17:20-21, 19:39; Acts 5:33-42).

[12] Once again, we have reason to be suspicious. Just as in Matthew, certain elements of Luke's birth account do not appear to be straight reporting but reflections of the author's own habits of thought, as expressed in the rest of the Gospel and in the Acts of the Apostles (which was written by the author of Luke). The birth account displays the author's ongoing interest in John the Baptist, whose work he will describe in detail (Luke 3:1-20, 7:18-35; Acts 1:5,22, 10:37, 11:16, 13:24-25, 18:25, 19:3-4); his pronounced theme of reversal (Luke 1:53; cf. 6:21-25); his preservation of a classic Jewish messianic hope, according to which Jesus will ultimately restore the throne to Israel (Luke 1:33,74; cf. Acts 1:6); and his unique connection of Christian origins with external political events (cf. Luke 3:1).

[13] Josephus, *The Jewish War* 2.117-118; *Antiquities of the Jews* 18.1-11.

[14] The classic discussion of the well-known historical issues related to the census is in Emil Schürer, *The History of the Jewish People in the Age of Jesus Christ*, ed. Geza Vermes et al., 3 vol. in 4 (Edinburgh: T & T Clark, 1973-1987), vol. 1, pp. 399-427.

[15] Most striking is the absence of Bethlehem from Acts. There the author of Luke takes every opportunity to use Old Testament scriptures to prove to Jewish audiences that Jesus was the Messiah (e.g., Acts 2:22-36, 4:8-30, 7:2-53, 13:16-43). Micah 5:2 would have been an obvious choice.

Where was Jesus Born?

JEROME MURPHY-O'CONNOR

STEVE MASON HAS PROBABLY MADE THE BEST CASE possible that we should adopt an "agnostic" position regarding the birthplace of Jesus. But although Mason has examined the literary data with exemplary care, he has failed to demolish the Gospels' conviction that Jesus was born in Bethlehem in the days of Herod the king. He has not even succeeded in bringing it into doubt.

Mason begins by saying that all the available evidence relating to the place of Jesus' birth must be taken into consideration before any location can be identified. I could not agree more. But the way Mason applies this principle does not inspire confidence. The archaeological evidence he presents is inadequate and dismissed far too quickly: "There is none," Mason claims. The Church of the Nativity, which still stands in Bethlehem, is irrelevant to Mason, who claims that Constantine probably selected the site of the church on the basis of the opening chapters of Matthew and Luke. But this is certainly wrong: We do have archaeological evidence from the Church of the Nativity.

The key factor in determining where the church

A ROCKY CAVE provides shelter for the infant Jesus in "Saint Bridget and Her Vision of the Nativity," by the 14th-century Italian artist Niccoló di Tommaso. In the painting, Bridget (c. 1302-1373), the patron saint of Sweden, kneels at right. Bridget, who spent the latter half of her life on pilgrimages to Rome and the Holy Land, claimed to receive visions from Mary of the birth and passion of Jesus. These apparitions incorporate details from early Christian apocryphal texts that did not make it into the New Testament but were nevertheless widely read and illustrated.

The cave setting recalls the *Protoevangelium of James*, a second-century gospel in which Mary is overcome by labor pains en route to Bethlehem, and Joseph must direct her to the nearest private spot—a cave. It also recalls local Bethlehem tradition, which, since at least the second century A.D., has identified a Bethlehem cave (now beneath the Church of the Nativity) as the spot where Jesus was born. Jerome Murphy-O'Connor, the author of the accompanying article, argues that these early local traditions and apocryphal gospels, along with the independent witnesses of Matthew and Luke, support Bethlehem as the place of Jesus' birth.

Bethlehem
... Of Course

should be built was a venerated cave, which lies beneath the apse of the church today (see photos, pp. 20-21). The cave is not mentioned either by Matthew or by Luke but appears in several other early Christian texts. According to the Christian apologist Justin Martyr (100-165 A.D.), when Joseph could not find room at the inn, "he moved into a certain cave near the village, and while they were there Mary brought forth the Christ and placed him in a manger."[1] Justin's information must derive from a specific Bethlehem tradition, which as a native of Palestine (he was born about 40 miles to the north, in Flavia Neapolis, modern Nablus), Justin was in a position to hear.

Some might argue that Justin invented the cave to fulfill a prophecy of Isaiah: "He [the Lord interpreted by Christians as the Christ] shall dwell in a lofty cavern of a strong rock" (Isaiah 33:16). But it is improbable that Justin invented the tradition. Justin would never have created a story that might lead his readers to conflate Jesus with the pagan deity Mithra, who was said to have been born from a rock and was worshiped in cave temples throughout the Roman world in Jesus' time.* Elsewhere, Justin shows that he is fully aware of the danger of parallels being drawn between Jesus and Mithra.

The tradition of Jesus' birth in a cave was also known independently to the anonymous second-century A.D. author of the *Protoevangelium of James*. According to this noncanonical gospel, Joseph and a pregnant Mary were traveling to Bethlehem when Mary cried, "Take me down from the ass, for the child within me presses me, to come forth."

Joseph asked, "Where shall I take you and hide your shame? For the place is a desert." Joseph guided Mary into a nearby cave, where she gave birth. Later, a brilliant star directed the Magi to the cave.[2]

The Protoevangelium author's ignorance of the geography of Palestine (for example, he thought the cave was outside Bethlehem) suggests that he was a native of, perhaps, Egypt or Syria. He must have heard about the cave from returning travelers.

That the cave had become the focus of

pilgrimage is confirmed by the early church father Origen (185-254 A.D.), who reports that "there is shown at Bethlehem the cave where he [Jesus] was born."[3] The cave apparently attracted regular visitors, including Origen himself sometime between 231 and 246 A.D.

It is difficult to imagine that the Bethlehemites invented the cave tradition, particularly because, as there is reason to suspect, the cave was not always accessible to Christians in the days of Justin and Origen. According to the church father Jerome (342-420 A.D.), who lived in Bethlehem from 386 A.D. until his death, the cave had been converted into a shrine dedicated to Adonis: "From Hadrian's time [135 A.D.] until the reign of Constantine, for about 180 years ... Bethlehem, now ours, and the earth's, most sacred spot ... was overshadowed by a grove of Thammuz,** which is Adonis, and in the cave where the infant Messiah once cried, the paramour of Venus was bewailed."[4]

Local Christians were probably not permitted to worship regularly in what had become a pagan shrine. The fact that the Bethlehemites did not simply select another site as the birth cave suggests that they did not feel free to invent. They were bound to a specific cave.[5] To preserve a local memory for almost 200 years implies a very strong motivation, a motivation that has nothing to do with the Gospels. With this in mind, let us evaluate the texts cited by Mason.

All that Mason says about the silence of Paul, Acts, Mark, John and some Jewish and Roman historians who fail to mention Jesus' birthplace is irrelevant. Deductions from silence will appeal only to those who have already made up their minds. The most that we can derive from these sources is that Jesus was believed to have come from Nazareth. Therefore, we must focus exclusively on those two writers who do mention his birthplace—Matthew and Luke.

Mason has well brought out that Matthew and Luke offer us "irreconcilably different" accounts of Jesus' birth: For Matthew, the story begins in Bethlehem, where Mary and Joseph live; Herod's slaughter of the innocents forces the family to move to Egypt, then on to Nazareth. In Luke, however, the family lives in Nazareth and only travels to Bethlehem for a census, at which time Jesus is born. What Mason fails to appreciate, however, is that Matthew 1-2 and Luke 1-2 are

---

*Mithraism was a mystery religion that arose in the Mediterranean world at the same time as Christianity. Temples to the god Mithra, who was thought to have sprung from the rock, were built underground, in imitation of caves. See David Ulansey, "Solving the Mithraic Mysteries," *Biblical Archaeology Review*, September/October 1994.

**Thammuz is an Eastern pagan deity associated with Adonis.

completely independent witnesses. One does not borrow from the other, nor do they both draw on a common source. This only enhances the reliability of the points on which they agree. According to Matthew, "Jesus was born in Bethlehem of Judea in the days of Herod the king" (2:1). Luke mentions "the days of Herod, king of Judea" (1:5) as the period of the annunciation of the birth of John the Baptist, which was separated from that of Jesus by only a few months. Jesus' birth took place after a journey "to Judea, to the city of David, which is called Bethlehem" (2:4). The two evangelists, therefore, independently confirm each other as to the time and place of Jesus' birth.

With regard to Matthew's birth narrative (Matthew 1-2), Mason asks whether the evangelist might have written Jesus' story in a way that makes it seem to fulfill Old Testament prophecy. Mason points out that at the end of each movement in Matthew's birth narrative we find a quotation from the Old Testament introduced by a formula emphasizing the idea of fulfillment: "All this took place to fulfill what had been spoken by the Lord through the prophet" (Matthew 1:22, 2:5,15,17,23). Mason asks: "Is it more likely that the author included a Bethlehem birth for Jesus because he knew that this had in fact happened or because he knew of the passage in scripture ["But you, O Bethlehem, ... from you shall come forth for me one who is to rule in Israel" (Micah 5:1-3 = Matthew 2:6)] and thought it important to describe Jesus' career in the language of the prophets?" Mason invites the reader to accept the second option by showing (quite accurately) how, later in the gospel, Matthew tends to adjust

A FAMILY TREE worth boasting about. To establish Jesus as the Messiah, both Matthew and Luke list his genealogy—as far back as Abraham in the former and all the way to Adam in the latter. In both versions, the lineage passes through David, the tenth-century B.C. king of Israel. This 12th-century A.D. window from the Cathedral of Chartres traces the multiple generations from David's grandfather Jesse, who reclines at the bottom, to Jesus himself. The stained-glass Tree of Jesse illustrates Isaiah 11:1-3: "A shoot shall come out from the stump of Jesse, and a branch shall grow out of his roots. The spirit of the Lord shall rest on him"—a prediction that the Messiah will come from the House of David.

But, as Jerome Murphy-O'Connor, points out, the Davidic Messiah was also expected to be a fearsome warrior-king— the antithesis of Jesus. That Jesus was nevertheless identified as the Davidic Messiah indicates that where he was from—David's hometown of Bethlehem—mattered more than how he behaved.

The Church of the Nativity

The small, unassuming entrance (left) to the Church of the Nativity (far right) in Bethlehem belies the importance of this site to Christianity. The infant Jesus is said to have been born here, in a small cave beneath the floor of the church. Today, a golden star in the cave floor (center) marks the traditional spot of Jesus' birth.

The first Christian emperor, Constantine, had the original Church of the Nativity constructed above the site. Dedicated on May 31, 339 B.C., Constantine's church consisted of a square hall (about 90 feet on each side) divided by four rows of columns into a hall with four aisles. At the northeastern end of the church, directly above the cave, was a raised octagonal apse, each side of which was 15 feet long. Pilgrims could view the cave through a 13-foot-wide hole in the center of the apse floor.

In the late fourth century, the church father Jerome moved to Bethlehem, where he translated the Old and New Testaments into Latin—a translation known as the Vulgate because it was done in the "vulgar," or "common," language of his day. Legend has it that Jerome used one of the caves beneath the church (adjacent to the nativity cave) as his study.

The church was at least partially razed in the sixth century by the Byzantine emperor Justinian, who then built a larger edifice on Constantine's foundations. Justinian had his builders imitate the style of the original church's columns, leading many modern investigators to believe that all of the capitals date to Constantine. Since Justinian's day, only a few changes have been made to the building, in spite of earthquake and fire.

the story of Jesus' life based on certain Old Testament prophesies. For example, Matthew's version of Jesus entering Jerusalem on the back of a donkey and its colt (Matthew 21:1-9) is strongly influenced by the prophecy of Zechariah 9:9 ("Lo, your king comes to you; triumphant and victorious is he, humble and riding on a donkey, on a colt, the foal of a donkey").

But does this mean that Jesus never rode into Jerusalem? Of course not! Matthew's primary source for the episode of the entry into Jerusalem is Mark 11:1-10, which describes Jesus riding into Jerusalem on a colt. It was this story in Mark that led Matthew to use Isaiah 62:11 and Zechariah 9:9 to bring out the significance of the event. In other words, an event evoked the prophecy; the prophecy was not the source of the event, even though it did influence the way it was presented in Matthew's later gospel.

This example of Matthew's literary technique establishes the way each of the "fulfillment"

prophecies in the first two chapters in his gospel must be approached. Matthew's source(s) triggered recollections of Old Testament prophecies, which Matthew then incorporated when he rewrote the story. One cannot seriously imagine an evangelist thumbing his way through his sacred scriptures in search of quotations on which to embroider a story. Simple common sense tells us it was much more a question of "Hey! That reminds me of something in Isaiah!"

For the sake of argument, I will accept Mason's claims that the episodes involving the "mysterious star" guiding the Magi (Matthew 2:1-12) and Herod's massacre of the innocents (Matthew 2:16-18) are not historical.[6] But what has this to do with the gospel's unequivocal and unexceptional assertion that Jesus was born in Bethlehem? Mason invites his readers to assume that all the details in Matthew's birth narrative are fabricated simply because these two episodes are fabricated. But falsehood is

PHOTOS BY GARO NALBANDIAN

not a toxic gas that affects everything around it.

Now let us turn to Luke. Mason recognizes (as do all scholars) that the census mentioned in Luke (2:1-2) took place in 6 A.D., which is far too late to be of any relevance to the birth of Jesus in the days of Herod the king (37-4 B.C.): In other words, Joseph and Mary could not have been traveling to Bethlehem for this census. Thus, the linchpin of Luke's narrative slips out, and the story fragments into a number of individual, unrelated elements. But the fact that Luke is wrong on X (the census) does not necessarily mean that he is wrong on Y (the location of Jesus' birth).

Finally, we come to Mason's conclusions. Mason's reason for evoking New Testament documents such as Mark and Paul, which say nothing about the birthplace of Jesus, only now becomes apparent. In Mason's view, the silence of these writers indicates that "it was fairly late when some Christians first became more interested in

the question [of where Jesus had been born]." Now, it might be fairly late when some Christians wrote about the birthplace of Jesus, but that says nothing about when they first became interested in or knowledgeable about the subject.

Mason continues, "Even by the time of Matthew and Luke, reliable information about Jesus' birth was no longer available." Nothing in his article lays the ground for such a statement. Matthew and Luke are unreliable on some points, but Mason has not demonstrated that the birthplace of Jesus is one of them.

Assuming that reliable information was unavailable to Matthew and Luke, Mason postulates that one of their sources created the story: "These authors [Matthew and Luke] took the basic proposition (probably from an earlier, now-lost source) that Jesus, the son of David, had been born in Bethlehem before Joseph and Mary had become intimate. This proposition could easily have originated in reflection upon Micah 5:2."

The idea that birth narratives as different as those of Matthew and Luke could go back to a common source boggles the mind. It would have been most interesting to see Mason even begin to attempt to outline the contents of such a source. Matthew, as we have seen, did not generate events on the basis of prophecy. On the contrary, he used prophecies to bring out the meaning of events otherwise attested. There is no hint that Micah 5:2 was of any importance for Luke. It is implausible, therefore, to infer that he derived his choice of Jesus' birthplace from this prophecy. Nor did he derive it from Matthew, whose version of the childhood of Jesus he did not know. The one option left is that Luke knew it for a fact.

One concluding observation: Mason claims that "establishing some kind of connection with David might have been critical for a messianic figure ... in Jesus' time." He writes: "A birth in Bethlehem, King David's place of origin, would naturally cement Jesus' Jewish messianic affiliation." But during Jesus' lifetime, belief that he was the Messiah did not require seeing him as the son of David (and therefore did not benefit from any connection with Bethlehem). In this period, the Davidic Messiah was not the only type of Messiah hoped for. Priest, prophet and teacher figures were also expected.[7] It would have been much easier for a contemporary to have fitted Jesus into any one of these categories. (Remember, his mother was related to Elizabeth, a descendant of Aaron, the first priest [Luke 1:5,36].) None of these other messianic categories had any connection with Bethlehem. In consequence, Jesus could have been thought of as a Messiah without any reference to Bethlehem.

Furthermore, of the many different categories of Messiah, that of Davidic Messiah would have been the least likely match for Jesus in the eyes of his contemporaries. Indeed, Jesus' behavior was the antithesis of that of a son of David, who was expected to be a warrior king who would rule with supreme authority. This hope is expressed most vividly in the first-century B.C. *Psalms of Solomon*:

> See, Lord, and raise up for them their king, the Son of David, to rule over your servant Israel in the time known to you, O God. Undergird him with the strength to destroy the unrighteous rulers, to purge Jerusalem from Gentiles who trample her to destruction; in wisdom and in righteousness to drive out the sinners from the inheritance; to smash the arrogance of sinners like a potter's jar; to shatter all their substance with an iron rod; to destroy the unlawful nations with the word of his mouth.[8]

Jesus, on the contrary, was the friend of tax collectors and sinners. He made no move against the Roman occupiers or the absentee landlords. He had no political agenda, and his compassion for the poor and disadvantaged was individual, not national. Moreover, he seems to have reacted against the idea of a royal Messiah.[9]

If the early church thought of Jesus in terms of Davidic messianism—and it certainly did[10]—it was not because of anything he said or did but because of who he was and where he came from. And he came from Bethlehem. ◪

[1] Justin Martyr, *Dialogue with Trypho* 78.6. The term apologist refers to early Christian writers who tried to defend and promote their faith in their writings. In his *Dialogue with Trypho*, Justin Martyr explains why he believes Jesus should be understood as the Messiah of the Old Testament.

[2] *Protoevangelium of James* 17-21, quoted in Wilhelm Schneemelcher, ed., *New Testament Apocrypha*, vol. 1, *Gospels and Related Writings*, rev. ed., English trans. ed. by R. McWilson (Tübingen: Mohr, 1990; Cambridge, UK: James Clark Louisville, KY: Westminster John Knox, 1991), pp. 433-435.

[3] Origen, *Contra Celsum* 1.51.

[4] Jerome, *Epistle* 58.

[5] For the location of the cave in the first-century town, see Shemaryahu Gutman and A. Berman, "Bethléem," *Revue biblique* 77 (1970), pp. 583-585. The excavation of the cave is reported by Benjamin Baggati, "Recenti Scavi a Betlemme," *Liber Annuus* 18 (1968), pp. 181-237.

[6] Nevertheless, I disagree with Mason's reading of both accounts. In both instances Mason's approach is decidedly unsophisticated. He is oblivious to the distinction between source and redaction in Matthew 2:1-12 and fails to appreciate the real import of Matthew 2:16-18, which is revealed by the "fulfillment" quotation of Jeremiah 31:15. This citation focuses on Ramah, which for Jeremiah (40:1) was the place where the Jews to be deported to Babylon were assembled. The slaughter of the babies has much more to do with the flight into Egypt than with Bethlehem itself.

[7] See John J. Collins, *The Scepter and the Star: The Messiahs of the Dead Sea Scrolls and Other Ancient Literature* (New York: Doubleday, 1995), p. 209; William Horbury, *Jewish Messianism and the Cult of Christ* (London: SCM, 1998).

[8] *Psalms of Solomon* 17.21-24. For this theme in other texts, see Collins, *Scepter and the Star*, pp. 49-73.

[9] See J.D.G. Dunn, "Messianic Ideas and Their Influence on the Jesus of History," in *The Messiah: Developments in Earliest Judaism and Christianity*, ed. James H. Charlesworth (Minneapolis, MN: Fortress, 1992), pp. 373-376.

[10] See John P. Meier, *A Marginal Jew—Rethinking the Historical Jesus*, vol. 1, *The Roots of the Problem and the Person* (New York: Doubleday, 1991), pp. 216-219.

Response & Surresponse

WE INVITED PROFESSOR MASON to respond to Professor Murphy-O'Connor's comments on the preceding pages, and he agreed. We then asked Professor Murphy-O'Connor to respond to Professor Mason. He too agreed. Their statements appear below:

Steve Mason's response:

Polemicists and apologists attach themselves to conclusions; they either attack them or defend them. Historians, on the other hand, pose open-ended questions, asking When? Where? and especially, Why?

Although I did my best to cast my essay on where Jesus was born in the historical mode, much of Professor Murphy-O'Connor's critique suggests that he imagined it as polemical. Clarification may be in order.

Despite appearances, what Murphy-O'Connor and I agree on is much more extensive—and important—than what we disagree on. In particular, we concur that the early Christians were quite creative with historical details of Jesus' life. He notes that the census mentioned in Luke 2:1 cannot have been the occasion for Jesus' birth in Bethlehem, and he acknowledges that Matthew created historical details (the Magi, the massacre of the innocents) to suit his Gospel's agenda. Like the other writers, Luke felt quite free to change times and events, placing, for example, the census of 6 A.D. during the reign of Herod (37-4 B.C.).

Second, Murphy-O'Connor and I agree that the earliest surviving evidence for Jesus' birth is relatively late, as much as 100 years after the event. We apparently disagree as to how far back one can trace, by inference, the roots of this evidence. These two points of agreement (the historical inaccuracies and the late date of our earliest witnesses) are the basis of my argument.

The logic of my essay was fairly straightforward. In answer to the question "Where was Jesus born?" I wished to determine whether there was sufficient evidence to support a probable hypothesis. The answer, it seems to me, must be "no." We have no firsthand evidence. We must depend on those who were in a position to know. But Jesus and his family members left nothing in writing. The first generation of Jesus' followers, reflected in Paul's letters, is similarly silent. Only in the second and third generations, 60 to 120 years after the event (the time of the gospel evidence), do we find implicit and explicit statements concerning Jesus' birthplace. These are in some tension, however. Mark and John suggest a Nazarene origin and Matthew and Luke both name Bethlehem as Jesus' birthplace—but under very different circumstances. By the fourth generation, the birth stories of Matthew and Luke had become widely known and to a large extent conflated. References to Jesus' birth in a cave, as mentioned by Murphy-O'Connor, appear only in this fourth generation; the first Church of the Nativity is erected even later, in the fourth century. This evidence is not of sufficiently high quality to permit a probable historical judgment about Jesus' birthplace.

If Murphy-O'Connor wished to make a Bethlehem hypothesis historically probable, he would need to demonstrate not only that the evidence is of high enough quality to support a probable judgment, but that the Bethlehem hypothesis best explains all the evidence. He would need to explain how we know that the Bethlehem element of the Matthean and Lukan birth stories originates with Jesus or his immediate family, while other elements on which they disagree—the census (Luke) or the persecution by Herod (Matthew), the family's origin in Nazareth (Luke) or Bethlehem (Matthew), and other elements—do not. He would need to ask: Was the Bethlehem story widely known among Jesus' first followers? If it was, why did Mark and John suggest (or imply) a Nazarene origin? Why are the accounts of Matthew and Luke so contradictory, as Murphy-O'Connor admits? Explaining all the relevant evidence this way is indispensable to making historical hypotheses probable or even plausible. Strangely, Murphy-O'Connor bypasses this task altogether and dismisses as "irrelevant" my attempt to consider the germane evidence from our earliest, silent sources (Paul, Mark, Acts, etc.).

In lieu of examining the earliest evidence, he argues that the local Bethlehem tradition about Jesus' cave-manger goes back to at least the mid-second century A.D. and Justin Martyr (wrote c. 150 A.D.). Murphy-O'Connor seems to think that this is relevant archaeological evidence for Jesus' birth, since he chides me for ignoring it. Fascinating though the cave tradition may be, only one thing about it is relevant to us: Is this tradition, which appears 150 years after Jesus' birth, more easily explained as a continuous and independent recollection of Jesus' birth in Bethlehem or as a later tradition that developed

on the basis of the birth stories in Matthew and Luke? If, as Murphy-O'Connor suggests, there was a continuous and vigorous tradition in Bethlehem about Jesus' birth (before Herod's death in 4 B.C.) that predates the Gospels, it would be very difficult to explain Mark, John, Matthew and Luke—including the dramatically different stories in the last two concerning how Jesus came to be born in Bethlehem.

Murphy-O'Connor's basic position is that my analysis amounts to "deductions from silence." Here he makes an elementary error. Arguments from silence are bad because they falsely deduce

...because those who were in a position to know did not speak clearly about the place of Jesus' birth, we cannot hope to be clear on the matter.

a conclusion from ambiguity. If one were to assert—against a Bethlehem birth—that because first-generation Christians were silent about the Bethlehem birth they could not have known of it, that would indeed be a fallacious argument from silence. Or if one were to maintain—in support of a Bethlehem birth—that the first-generation authors were silent because they assumed he was born in Bethlehem, that too would be fallacious. In either case, one would be deducing a positive conclusion from ambiguous silence.

Since my argument did not reach any such positive conclusion, however, but gave the deafening silence its full weight, I cannot be charged with arguing from silence. Please recall: I said that because those who were in a position to know did not speak clearly about the place of Jesus' birth, we cannot hope to be clear on the matter. To support the Bethlehem hypothesis (or any other) as historically probable would require an argument from silence—that the first-generation authors as well as Mark and John knew about it, even though they did not mention it. Thus Murphy-O'Connor contends: "Now, it might be fairly late when some Christians wrote about the birthplace of Jesus, but that says nothing about when they first became interested in or knowledgeable about the subject."

I reject all such arguments from silence.

Murphy-O'Connor has the right principle but the wrong target.

One small point: Murphy-O'Connor's mind is boggled, he says, that I should attribute the agreement of Matthew and Luke on Bethlehem (and on precious little else) to a "source." My mind is boggled by his boggled mind. When two authors agree on something, there are only three possibilities. Either they independently and coincidentally invented the item; or one borrowed it from the other (or they colluded) directly or through mediation; or they independently got it from some third party. We would presumably all agree that Matthew and Luke did not likely invent the Bethlehem location out of thin air, coincidentally. And Murphy-O'Connor supports the common view that they wrote independently of one another. That leaves only the possibility that their agreement on Bethlehem goes back to some third party, to some other source. Perhaps Murphy-O'Connor imagines that I meant a shared written source, but I neither said nor intended such a thing.

Murphy-O'Connor rightly notes that the Christians' identification of Jesus as Messiah did not require them to create a Bethlehem birth, since even the notion that the Messiah should be a descendant of David was only one option among many in ancient Judaism. I said much the same: As far as we know, most other Jews did not expect a Messiah born in Bethlehem. Mark, in a story taken over by Matthew, even has Jesus challenging the notion that the Messiah should be David's descendant (Mark 12:35-37). Nevertheless, in an ancient context that preferred its distinguished persons to have distinguished births, it was natural that some Christians would explore the manner of Jesus' birth long after the fact. For Christians with such an outlook, the connection with David and with scripture fulfillment would be a sufficient (not necessary) point of origin for the Bethlehem tradition. There was nothing requiring the author of Matthew to have Jesus fulfill scripture by visiting Egypt or by riding two animals (as he understood the Messiah would do from the prophet Zechariah), but Matthew did write under this influence. Matthew did not include only those elements he knew to have happened historically.

Jerome Murphy-O'Connor is a highly respected scholar, and I regard his work with the greatest admiration. On the question of Jesus'

birthplace he poses provocative questions about the backdating of the Bethlehem cave tradition and the notices in Matthew and Luke. At the end of the day, however, we all run up against the silence of the only ones clearly in a position to know. Murphy-O'Connor has not shown why Jesus' birth in Bethlehem is more than a mere possibility.—S.M.

Jerome Murphy-O'Connor's surresponse:

The difference between Professor Mason and me boils down to the way we approach ancient texts in search of historical information. He treats the Gospels as defendants with a poor record of veracity. What the authors say must be treated with the gravest suspicion because the likelihood is that they made it up, particularly if the texts are of late date. Inevitably he comes to the conclusion that we cannot know what happened.

I, on the contrary, treat the Gospels as witnesses. They may be confused and biased, they may rely on inaccurate information, but their aim is to tell the truth. Thus when the Gospels offer me what appears to be historical information, I accept it at face value, unless I have proof to the contrary.

Thus Mason rejects Bethlehem as the birthplace of Jesus because he can find no reason to accept it, but I accept that Jesus was born in Bethlehem because I find no reason to reject it.

Which of these approaches is to be preferred? Mine is simply the application to the Gospels of the method human beings use in dealing with all sources of information, both ancient and modern. We believe what we are told, or read, unless we have reason to be suspicious about it. We do not automatically ask for proof of truth, but we are instinctively alert for false notes. Information flows in unless it is blocked by a critical sieve.

If Mason's approach to the Gospels reflects the way he lives, he must be "agnostic" about everything. I doubt very much that this is in fact the case. Life would be impossible. Which means, of course, that he singles out the Gospels for uniquely harsh treatment as sources of historical knowledge. This is unjustifiable. The Gospels must be treated as all other documents. Mason may think that he is acting as a responsible historian, but in his approach, criticism, which might yield positive results, has been transformed into skepticism, which is a dead end.—J.M-O'C. ■

Has Jesus' Nazareth Hou Been Found?

KEN DARK

WHAT WAS NAZARETH LIKE WHEN Jesus lived there? The evidence is sparse but intriguing.

Surprising as it may seem, very little archaeological work has been done in Nazareth itself. However, a site within the Sisters of Nazareth Convent, across the street from the Church of the Annunciation, may contain some of the best evidence of the small town that existed here in Jesus' time. Although known since the 1880s, this had never previously been properly published or even studied by professional archaeologists—until the Nazareth Archaeological Project began work here in 2006.[1]

The story begins with the chance discovery of an ancient cistern in the 1880s,

KEN DARK

se

KEN DARK

HOME OF JESUS? Pictured (previous pages) is the rock-cut doorway of the first-century h ouse at the Sisters of Nazareth Convent. The combination of rock-built construction and quarried-rock construction can be seen clearly. The door opens to the "Chambre Obscure," another part of the original house structure partly cut out of the natural rock. The rock overhang in the corner is naturally occurring and was likely left in its current form to support the roof. In front of the doorway, a fragment of the original floor survives. The east side of the structure (above) originally had rock built walls, as this part of the house was built away from the naturally occurring rock cave. The visible wall was rebuilt in the Crusader period but may incorporate remains of the first-century A.D. wall.

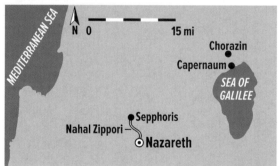

shortly after the convent was built. Excavations were then undertaken by the nuns, their workmen and even children from their school. They exposed a complex sequence of unusually well preserved archaeological features, including Crusader-period walls and vaults, a Byzantine cave-church, Roman-period tombs and other rock-cut and built structures. The nuns made a small museum of the pottery, coins, glass and other portable artifacts that they recovered. Then construction of the new convent buildings revealed the walls of a large Byzantine church with a triple apse, polychrome mosaic floors and white marble fittings, rebuilt in the Crusader period.

Did all this ancient construction, including churches and burials, indicate that the site was considered holy, or at least of some importance, at various periods after Jesus' time? Was this perhaps founded on a belief that the site was somehow related to Jesus' home?

In 1936, the Jesuit Father Henri Senès, who had been an architect before entering the Church, recorded the previously exposed structures in great detail and undertook some further, though limited, excavations. Unfortunately Senès never published his work (apart from a brief guide pamphlet). But he did leave a substantial archive of notes and drawings, little known outside the convent, to which the nuns have graciously given us access.

In 2006, we began to reexamine the site. It soon became clear that there was a lengthy

ROTEM HOFMAN

ROTEM HOFMAN

WITHIN THE SISTERS OF NAZARETH CONVENT (above) is the first-century "courtyard house." While excavation in this area was initiated in 1880, it was not until the Nazareth Archaeological Project began their investigation in 2006 that the site was studied by professional archaeologists. A modern statue of the "Holy Family" (right) is featured in the courtyard of the convent, reflecting the nuns' belief that this was the location of the house in Nazareth where Jesus grew up.

chronological sequence of well-preserved structures and features. This included the successive Crusader and Byzantine churches, two Early Roman-period tombs, a phase of small-scale quarrying and, of particular note, a rectilinear structure with partly rock-cut and partly stone-built walls.

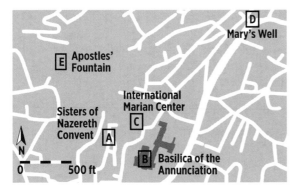

The rectilinear structure was cut through by the forecourt of a tomb dated to the first century; therefore the rectilinear structure must have been built earlier than this time. That this structure also dated to the Roman period was confirmed by the Kefar Hananya-type pottery (standard domestic pottery of Roman-period Galilee; see photo p. 34), the date of which is otherwise

NAZARETH. The excavation site in the cellar of the Sisters of Nazareth Convent (A) may reveal the childhood home of Jesus. Finds from this site and those in the vicinity of the Church of the Annunciation (B) and the International Marian Center (C) suggest that the town of Nazareth was somewhat larger and wealthier than often portrayed.

Ancient Nazareth was served by three to seven springs, two of which, the Apostles' Fountain (E) and Mary's Well (D), are still known.

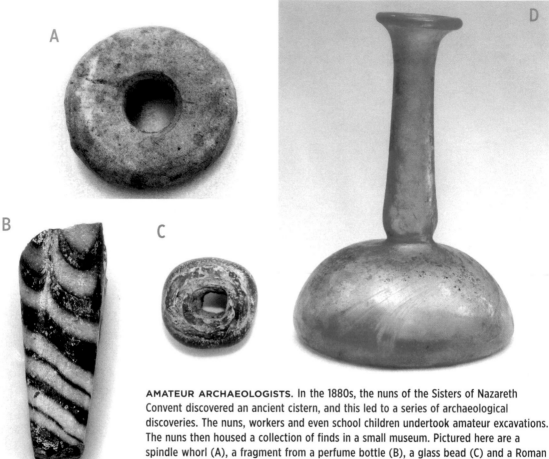

A

B

C

D

KEN DARK

AMATEUR ARCHAEOLOGISTS. In the 1880s, the nuns of the Sisters of Nazareth Convent discovered an ancient cistern, and this led to a series of archaeological discoveries. The nuns, workers and even school children undertook amateur excavations. The nuns then housed a collection of finds in a small museum. Pictured here are a spindle whorl (A), a fragment from a perfume bottle (B), a glass bead (C) and a Roman glass vase (D).

known.[2] Probable fragments of limestone vessels indicate that the inhabitants were very likely Jewish. Limestone vessels are not subject to impurity under Jewish law and were therefore very popular in Jewish communities at this time.

What sort of building was this rectilinear structure? It had been constructed by cutting back a limestone hillside as it sloped toward the wadi (valley) below, leaving carefully smoothed freestanding rock walls, to which stone-built walls were added. The structure included a series of rooms. One, with its doorway, survived to its full height. Another had a stairway rising adjacent to one of its walls. A rock overhang had been carefully retained in one room, its upper surface worked to support part of a roof or upper story—which otherwise must have been built of another material, probably timber. Just inside the surviving doorway, earlier excavations had revealed part of its original chalk floor. Associated finds, including cooking pottery and a spindle whorl, suggested domestic occupation.

Taken together, the walls conformed to the plan of a so-called courtyard house, one of the typical architectural forms of Early

Roman-period settlements in the Galilee.

The excellent preservation of this rectilinear structure or house can be explained by its later history. Great efforts had been made to encompass the remains of this building within the vaulted cellars of both the Byzantine and Crusader churches, so that it was thereafter protected.

Initially puzzling was the use of the site for Jewish burial. Although domestic occupation was of course prohibited by Jewish law on burial sites, burial on a disused domestic site was another matter. The burials were also separated from domestic occupation by a phase of quarrying. It is clear the house was already disused before the site was used for tombs. The immediate area was mostly destroyed before the tombs were constructed. Consequently, the apparent conflict between domestic occupation and burial is an illusory one. The house must date from the first century A.D. or earlier. No stratified pottery earlier or later than the Early Roman period was discovered in layers associated with the house.[3]

In 2009, another first-century courtyard house was discovered nearby—in a salvage (or rescue) excavation directed by Yardenna Alexandre of the Israel Antiquities Authority prior to the construction of the International Marian Center next to the Church of the Annunciation.[4] This reveals a structure similar to the Sisters of Nazareth house. The principal difference between the two structures is that the Marian Center structure has fewer rock-cut components as it was built on relatively flat ground farther away from the side of the hill.

Consequently, we now have two first-century courtyard houses from central Nazareth. These, together with the other earlier discoveries at the Church of the Annunciation, provide evidence for an Early Roman Jewish settlement that was larger, and perhaps slightly wealthier, than is often envisaged. Such evidence would be consistent with what archaeologists of the Roman provinces elsewhere conventionally term a "small town": a large village, perhaps perceived by contemporaries as a small urban center, serving as a focus for smaller agricultural communities nearby.

Nazareth was served by at least three, and possibly as many as seven, springs or wells. St. Mary's Well is perhaps the best known of these. Another is the so-called Apostles' Fountain near the modern Mensa Church. We found another spring in the course of our fieldwork at the Sisters of Nazareth Convent; it remains accessible through its Crusader-period wellhead. Another water source is implied by an unpublished plan of about 1900 in the convent archive, where a water channel is shown leading from the so-called Synagogue Church, north of the convent. According to Gottfried Schumacher, in the 19th century local

ROLLING TOMB STONE. The forecourt of this tomb cuts through the courtyard house that may have once been Jesus' home. Initially this was confusing, as Jewish law would not permit burials to take place near habitations, but the courtyard house had been abandoned prior to the installation of the tombs as evidenced by a period of quarrying. Both structures date to the first century A.D. The rock "door" would be similar to the stone that covered the entrance to the tomb of Jesus, which was rolled away at the resurrection (Mark 16:3; Matthew 28:2; Luke 24:2; John 20:1).

KEN DARK

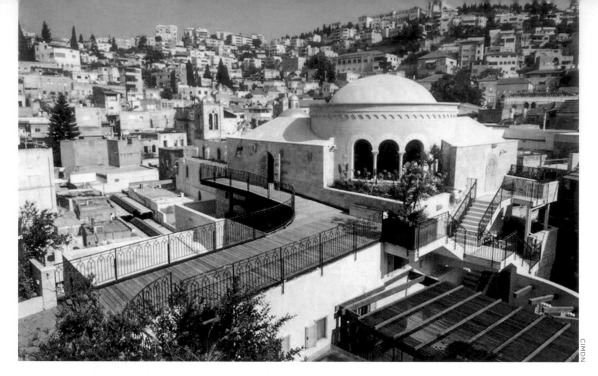

A RESCUE EXCAVATION done in 2009 prior to the construction of the International Marian Center, pictured here, revealed the remains of another first-century courtyard house from the time of Jesus. Featured in the photo is the dome of the center's chapel.

people knew of another spring located to the south.[5] The Palestine Exploration Fund's famous *Survey of Western Palestine* in the 1870s recorded a well within the Franciscan precinct of the Church of the Annunciation. Finally, in his 1923 *Das Land Der Bibel*, Paul Range says he saw another spring west of the Old City of Nazareth.

The hinterland of Nazareth is oriented to the north. To the south a high rocky ridge cuts off easy movement by foot or animal-drawn cart. To the north, however, a relatively gentle walk leads to the Nahal Zippori, the broad valley between Nazareth and the Roman town of Sepphoris (Zippori in Hebrew). This valley is well watered by the stream that flows along its center and by numerous springs and a few rivulets on its slopes. The part of Nahal Zippori closest to Nazareth was probably the agricultural hinterland of the settlement.

Between 2004 and 2010, the Nazareth Archaeological Project surveyed a wide transect across Nahal Zippori. We identified a series of previously unknown Early Roman-period sites, probably farms and small villages, which (with just two exceptions) had no pre-Roman material. At a few sites we also found evidence of quarrying.

It may be possible to say something of the cultural identity of those living in the Nahal Zippori at this time. All the sites on the south side of the valley, nearer to Nazareth, featured Kefar Hananya-type pottery. Some also had the type of limestone vessels associated elsewhere with Jewish settlements. However, all of those on the north side of the valley, nearer Sepphoris, had a much wider range of artifacts, including red-slipped imported Eastern Terra Sigillata pottery and imported amphora. Communities closer to Sepphoris apparently embraced the cultural world of the Roman provinces; those closer to Nazareth chose a strictly Jewish material culture, perhaps denoting a more conservative attitude to religious belief and concepts of purity and rejecting "Roman" culture as a whole.*

Nowhere else in the Roman Empire is there such a seemingly clear-cut boundary between people accepting and those rejecting Roman culture, even along the imperial Roman frontiers. This suggests that the Nazareth area was unusual for the strength of its anti-Roman sentiment and/or the strength of its Jewish identity. It also suggests that there was no close connection between Nazareth and Sepphoris in the Early Roman period. Perhaps these places occupied focal roles in separate "settlement systems" on either side of the valley.

Some recent scholarship has argued that the Roman culture of Sepphoris, closer than 5 miles from Nazareth, would have played an important part in Jesus' youth. Sepphoris, with its shop-lined

*Eric M. Meyers, "The Pools of Sepphoris: Ritual Baths or Bathtubs? Yes, They Are," *Biblical Archaeology Review,* July/August 2000; Mark Chancey and Eric M. Meyers, "Spotlight on Sepphoris: How Jewish Was Sepphoris in Jesus' Time?" *Biblical Archaeology Review,* July/August 2000; Zeev Weiss, "The Sepphoris Synagogue Mosaic," *Biblical Archaeology Review,* September/October 2000.

streets, mosaic-floored townhouses and monumental public buildings, might initially appear to support this contention. But the Sepphoris seen by visitors today is largely a later construction. Very little of what is known of Sepphoris may be assigned with certainty to the early first century.

The first-century evidence that we do have from Sepphoris suggests an urban center with an administrative function, domestic occupation and public buildings. It may have been relatively cosmopolitan, in the sense that it was open to Roman provincial culture, but it remained a Jewish community.

ANOTHER COURTYARD HOUSE, although with a few differences from the courtyard house found underneath the Sisters of Nazareth Convent, was excavated near the International Marian Center by Yardenna Alexandre of the Israel Antiquities Authority. Across the street from the courtyard house is the Church of the Annunciation (top of photo).

CISTERNS built into the courtyard of the house allow the occupants regular, easy access to water. The opening to the cistern (below) is one of two that would have served the courtyard house. The watercolor reconstruction shows the cisterns in relation to the house.

ROTEM HOFMAN

By contrast, Nazareth was a local center without the trappings of Roman culture, perhaps analogous to nearby Capernaum or Chorazin in its facilities and scale, rather than to Sepphoris (which, incidentally, is not mentioned in the New Testament). The description in the Gospels of the Nazareth synagogue (Mark 6:1–6; Matthew 13:54–58; Luke 4:16–30) is exactly the sort of building we would expect in an Early Roman provincial "small town." Such a small town was also exactly the sort of place where one might

MARY'S WELL. Modern construction covers the ancient water source known as Mary's Well. It is one of three to seven wells that served the ancient town.

expect to find a rural craftsman—a *tekton* (Mark 6:3; Matthew 13:55)—like Joseph.

This evidence suggests that Jesus' boyhood was spent in a conservative Jewish community that had little contact with Hellenistic or Roman culture. (It is extremely unlikely to be the sort of place where, as some have argued, one would

EVERYDAY DISHES. Known as Kefar Hananya pottery, it is associated with Jewish settlements in the Galilee and is common in the area surrounding Nazareth. It is characterized by its warm orange-brown color and smooth thin walls. It gives a clink when bumped due to the hard firing process used to create it. The clay is dense and homogenous with rare inclusions of black or white.

HIGH CLASS. Eastern Terra Sigillata ware is smooth and shiny as well as elegantly designed. These elements made it appeal to the higher classes of society, which could afford to buy imported goods. As its name suggests, Eastern Terra Sigillata ware began to be produced in the eastern Mediterranean region around 200 B.C. On this vessel, the light-colored areas are modern plaster reconstructions.

ISRAEL ANTIQUITIES AUTHORITY

ISRAEL ANTIQUITIES AUTHORITY/PHOTO BY YOLOVITCH YAEL

ROMAN CULTURE BECOMES dominant in the later development of Sepphoris. Fourth- and fifth-century A.D. remains reveal elaborate architecture and mosaics with a distinctly Roman influence. Yet even at this stage Sepphoris still has a strong Jewish presence, as demonstrated in a zodiac mosaic, recovered in the fifth-century A.D. synagogue. Here (right), Scorpio is identified by its Hebrew name, *Akrab*, reflecting the adaptation of the signs of the zodiac to Jewish culture.

have encountered "cynic" philosophy.)

None of this, of course, has any explicit connection with Jesus. There is one possible connection, however. A seventh-century pilgrim account known as *De Locus Sanctis*, written by Adomnán of Iona, describes two large churches in the center of Nazareth. One is identifiable as the Church of the Annunciation, located just across the modern street from the Sisters of Nazareth Convent. The other stood nearby and was built over vaults that also contained a spring and the remains of two tombs, *tumuli* in Adomnán's "Insular Latin." Between these two tombs, Adomnán tells us, was the house in which Jesus was raised. From this is derived the more recent name for the church that Adomnán describes: the Church of the Nutrition, that is, "the church of the upbringing of Christ," the location of which has been lost.[6]

At the Sisters of Nazareth Convent there was evidence of a large Byzantine church with a spring and two tombs in its crypt. The first-century

STAYING PURE. Limestone vessels were common in first-century Israel because they were not subject to impurity according to Jewish law; thus a stone cup like the one pictured here could be continually reused rather than destroyed, unlike vessels of pottery that had contracted impurity.

house described at the beginning of this article, probably a courtyard house, stands between the two tombs. Both the tombs and the house were decorated with mosaics in the Byzantine period, suggesting that they were of special importance, and possibly venerated. Only here have we evidence for all the characteristics that *De Locus Sanctis* ascribes to the Church of the Nutrition, including the house.

Was this the house where Jesus grew up? It is impossible to say on archaeological grounds. On the other hand, there is no good archaeological reason why such an identification should be discounted. What we can say is that this building was probably where the Byzantine church builders believed Jesus had spent his childhood in Nazareth. ▣

[1] The Nazareth Archaeological Project is a British archaeological project, sponsored by the Palestine Exploration Fund and the Late Antiquity Research Group. The project is directed by the author.

[2] D. Adan-Bayewitz, "On the Chronology of the Common Pottery of Northern Roman Judaea/Palestine," in G.C. Bottini, L. di Segni and L.D. Chrupcala, eds., *One Land—Many Cultures: Archaeological Studies in Honour of Stanislao Loffreda OFM* (Jerusalem: Franciscan Printing Press, 2003).

[3] For further details, see Ken Dark, "Early Roman-Period Nazareth and the Sisters of Nazareth Convent," *The Antiquaries Journal* 92 (2012), p. 1.

[4] Y. Alexandre, *Mary's Well, Nazareth: The Late Hellenistic to the Ottoman Periods* (Jerusalem: Israel Antiquities Authority Report 49, 2012).

[5] G. Schumacher, "Recent Discoveries in Galilee," *Palestine Exploration Fund Quarterly Statement* 21 (1889), p. 68.

[6] The present Franciscan Church of St. Joseph (the "Church of St. Joseph's Workshop") within the Church of the Annunciation compound is a Crusader foundation with no evidence of an earlier church on its site.

How Jewish was Jesus' Galilee?

MARK A. CHANCEY

THE PENDULUM IS BEGINNING TO SWING BACK AGAIN. Before 20th-century archaeologists began uncovering it, Jesus' Galilee was generally considered rural Jewish terrain. Then archaeologists made some astounding finds. Excavations at Sepphoris, less than 4 miles from Jesus' hometown of Nazareth, revealed inscriptions in Greek, Roman architecture

and some breathtaking Greco-Roman art, including the famous mosaic dubbed by excavator Carol Meyers the "Mona Lisa of the Galilee." The "Mona Lisa" was part of a larger mosaic depicting a *symposium* (a dinner with ample alcohol) with the mythological hero Hercules and the god of wine, Dionysus, as guests.

Digs at other sites in Galilee uncovered similar finds. The scholarly community was surprised, impressed and excited, and naturally sought to incorporate this new information into their reconstructions of Jesus' Galilee. Some scholars argued that Greek complemented Aramaic as a language of daily use in Galilee, that Greco-Roman architecture dotted the landscape and that artistic depictions of emperors, deities and mythological heroes were common.

A Roman-style theater at Sepphoris raised the intriguing hypothesis that Jesus had actually attended it, watching classical dramas and comedies.*

Jesus was soon compared to Cynic philosophers, those wandering counter-cultural preachers found in many cities of the Roman empire.

Some studies proposed that in Jesus' time, many Galileans were gentiles, whether Greeks, Romans, Phoenicians, Arabs or others.

Now, however, as more detailed publication of archaeological finds have made

*Richard A. Batey, "Sepphoris: An Urban Portrait of Jesus," *Biblical Archaeology Review*, May/June 1992.

more systematic study possible, many of these views are being questioned. The pendulum is swinging back—at least a little. Few would dispute that Greco-Roman culture was certainly a part of Galilean life in Jesus' time, but it is important to put this into perspective. The region's cultural milieu must be dated very carefully, for it changed quite considerably from period to period. In short, in Jesus' time it was not so permeated by Greco-Roman culture as some scholars have previously proposed. Much of the archaeological evidence most widely relied upon reflects the Galilee not of the early first century C.E., but rather the Galilee of the second, third and fourth centuries C.E.

To understand the growth of Greco-Roman culture in Galilee, we must trace its historical development. By Jesus' time, Galilee's encounter with Hellenism (Greek culture) was centuries old, going back to the age of Alexander the Great, the Macedonian king who conquered Palestine and much of the rest of the Near East during his brief reign (c. 336–323 B.C.E.).

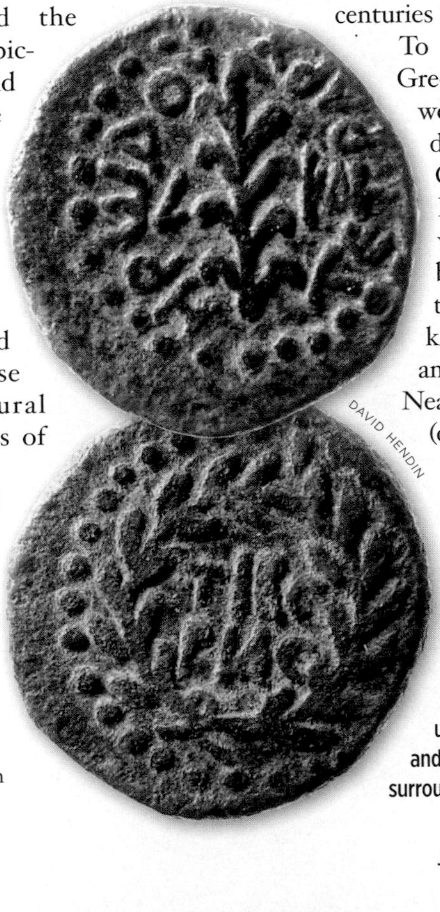

NO GRAVEN IMAGES. The coins from the reign of Herod Antipas have Greek inscriptions, but depict no living beings so as not to offend the sensibilities of the Jewish population. The coin shown here was struck during the 24th year of his reign, or 20 C.E. It shows a reed upright with the date on the obverse and an inscription reading "Tiberias" surrounded by a wreath on the reverse.

DAVID HENDIN

On Alexander's death his kingdom was divided between the Ptolemies in Egypt and the south, on the one hand, and the Seleucids in the north, on the other. Palestine, in the middle, often changed hands between the dueling dynasties. In the second century B.C.E., the Jewish Hasmonean dynasty—they of the Maccabees—ruled an independent Jewish kingdom, but the Hasmoneans turned out to be very devoted to Hellenistic culture as well.

In 63 B.C.E. Pompey interceded militarily to quell a Hasmonean conflict, thus ending the independent Jewish kingdom and bringing direct Roman rule to Palestine. Naturally the Romans brought with them their own culture. The mixture of Hellenistic and Roman influence

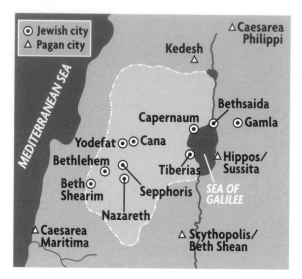

DRINK AND BE MERRY. After an apparently extended bout of drinking with Dionysus, the god of wine, an inebriated Hercules is aided by a maenad and a satyr. His club rests beside him and the Greek word for "drunkenness" appears above the shoulder of the satyr. This depiction of an ancient *symposium* is part of a larger mosaic floor of the third-century C.E. villa at Sepphoris.

The freely depicted graven images suggest that, by the late second and early third centuries, the population of Sepphoris included a significant number of gentiles. No such images have been found in these areas from the earlier time of Jesus.

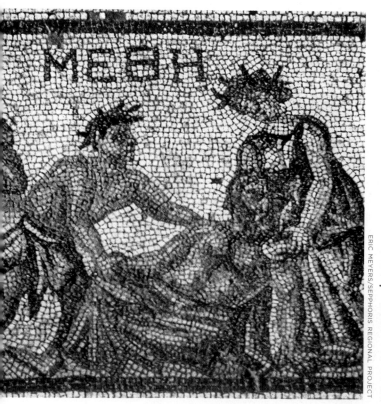

came to be known, naturally enough, as Greco-Roman culture.

In 40 B.C.E. the Romans installed a new king over the Jews of Palestine, Herod the Great. Herod is known from the New Testament as ordering the massacre of all the male infants in Bethlehem in hope of killing the baby Jesus (Matthew 2:16–18). Herod was a devoted and loyal patron of Greco-Roman culture not only in Palestine, but in the entire eastern Mediterranean world. Even outside his own territory, he sponsored numerous major building projects like gymnasia at Tripoli, Damascus and Ptolemais and theaters at Sidon and Damascus.[1] In Palestine he built two cities: Sebaste, on the site of Biblical Samaria, and Caesarea Maritima, his showcase port. Both cities had streets aligned on a grid, intersecting at right angles, which was characteristic of Greco-Roman cities. Caesarea Maritima boasted of agoras, an amphitheater (a round or oval theater for animal shows and combat sports), an aqueduct and a theater; all typical features of Greco-Roman culture.*

In Caesarea Maritima, Sebaste and Caesarea Philippi, Herod built temples to the emperor Augustus and Roma, goddess of the city of Rome (as well as rebuilding the Jewish Temple in Jerusalem).

Herod's largesse, however, does not seem to have extended to Galilee. Through the death of Herod the Great in 4 B.C.E., communities in

*See Robert J. Bull, "Caesarea Maritima: The Search for Herod's City," *Biblical Archaeology Review*, May/June 1982; Barbara Burrell, Kathryn Gleason and Ehud Netzer, "Uncovering Herod's Seaside Palace,"*Biblical Archaeology Review*, May/June 1993.

MARTY COOPER

Galilee appear to have remained without Greco-Roman architecture.

On his death, Herod's kingdom was divided. To his son Antipas (or Herod Antipas, also called "Herod" in the Gospels)[2] went Galilee. Antipas's rule lasted until 39 C.E., thus covering the life of Jesus.

Though his father had neglected the region, it was the center of Antipas's attention. He renamed Sepphoris Autocratoris, a name that honored the Roman emperor, whose Latin title of *Imperator* was translated into Greek as *Autocrator*.**[3] At least some of the city's streets were built on a grid pattern during his reign. The foundations of a basilical building—a rectangular, columned structure often used as a sort of "city hall" in Roman cities—may also date to his reign, as does one of the aqueduct systems. Some scholars (James F. Strange and Richard A. Batey) have dated Sepphoris's 4,500-person theater to

**See Mark Chancey and Eric M. Meyers, "How Jewish Was Sepphoris in Jesus' Time?" *Biblical Archaeology Review*, July/August 2000.

ALL THE WORLD'S A STAGE, but did Jesus ever see a play at the Sepphoris theater? Jesus often admonished his followers to be unlike the *hypocrites* (Matthew 6:2,5), a word that originally meant "one acting on the stage." It has been suggested that Jesus learned the word by attending stage presentations at Sepphoris, only 4 miles from Nazareth, where Jesus grew up. Herod Antipas completely rebuilt Sepphoris in the early first century as the crown and capital of his kingdom to compete with the grandeur of Rome after the death of his father, Herod the Great. Some scholars argue that Antipas would surely have included a theater in this project and date the 4,000-seat theater to Jesus' time based on pottery found underneath it. Other archaeologists believe that the theater was built decades after the crucifixion of Jesus.

Antipas's reign on the basis of pottery fragments discovered underneath the theater. Others (Carol and Eric Meyers, Zeev Weiss and Ehud Netzer) date this pottery and thus the theater above it to the late first or early second century C.E., after the crucifixion.[4] It is not yet clear whether a theater existed in Sepphoris that Jesus might have attended.

Everyone agrees, however, that at the end of

the first century, a period of extensive growth began in Sepphoris that continued for centuries. The grid pattern of the city's streets became even more pronounced, and a new aqueduct system (the one featured prominently in the modern park) was constructed, as were two Roman-style bathhouses.

As indicative as this is of Greco-Roman culture, it is also important to note what was not in the Galilee, although common in other areas of the Roman East at this time: no amphitheater, no gymnasium, no stadium and no nymphaeum (a large, elaborately decorated fountain).

The other major city in the Galilee (after Sepphoris) built by Antipas was Tiberias on the southwestern shore of the lake. Antipas founded it in about 20 C.E. and named it after the then-reigning Roman emperor, Tiberius (14–37 C.E.). The city underwent extensive growth in subsequent centuries, and the overlay of the modern resort city limits the area of potential excavation. Perhaps for these reasons, little has been

THE GREAT WINGS BEATING STILL, Zeus in the form of a swan comes to Leda and leaves her with child in this carving on a third- or fourth-century C.E. sarcophagus from the Jewish burial vaults at Beth She'arim. Artistic representations of animal and human figures can be found throughout the Galilee even in Jewish areas, but from after the time of Jesus. The decorations and artifacts that have been found in the region contemporaneous with Jesus are simple and generally do not depict living things.

recovered in modern excavations from the time of Antipas—and thus of Jesus as well. The Jewish historian Josephus refers to a sports stadium in Tiberias at the time of the First Jewish Revolt against Rome (66–70 C.E.),[5] and archaeologists may have found this structure.[6] As at Sepphoris, however, archaeologists have uncovered much Greco-Roman construction from later periods: a cardo (the main north-south street of Roman cities) in the second century; a theater in the second or third; and a bathhouse in the fourth.

At other Galilean sites, structures reflecting Greco-Roman culture veritably abound, but

"IN THE 34TH YEAR OF HEROD" reads the only inscription (aside from coins) yet found in the Galilee that dates to the lifetime of Jesus. In later years the frequency of inscriptions greatly increases, with Greek examples outnumbering those in Hebrew or Aramaic.

SHARAGA QEDAR

little if anything is from the first half of the first century. Roman-style bathhouses were found at Capernaum from the second or third century.* At the northern site of Rama, similar structures were found from the third or fourth century.[7] The situation is similar even with regard to synagogues. Synagogues from the fourth century onward reflect strong Greco-Roman architectural influence, as seen, for example, in their rectangular layouts and use of columns.

Communities near Galilee experienced similar developments. Scythopolis (Beth Shean), for example, on the southeastern border of Galilee, had an amphitheater, a bathhouse, a palaestra, a temple and possibly a nymphaeum—but all from the second century or later.**

The same chronological development we have seen with respect to Galilean architecture may also be observed in the visual arts—frescoes, mosaics, statues, figurines and funerary art. The interior walls of some first-century buildings were painted with geometric patterns: dots, lines and blocks of color. On the floors were some simple mosaics, often of only black and white

*See John C. H. Laughlin, "Capernaum: From Jesus' Time and After," *Biblical Archaeology Review*, September/October 1993.

**See "Glorious Beth-Shean," *Biblical Archaeology Review*, July/August 1990.

tesserae. Compare these rather basic decorations with the early-third-century Dionysus mosaic that included not only the Mona Lisa of the Galilee, but also panels depicting Dionysus (the Greek god of wine), his worshipers and entourage, and the mythical Hercules. Another panel portrays the wedding of Dionysus to Ariadne. Still another depicts bearers bringing gifts to the god. The mosaic is one of the highest quality found anywhere in Roman Palestine.[8] But it dates long after Jesus' time.

Other finds at Sepphoris from the second century and later likewise reflect an increasing comfort level with artistic depictions of humans, animals and deities, such

FROM THE TIBERIAS MINT. The coin shown at left depicts a bust of the emperor Hadrian, with a Roman boat and the word "Tiberias" on the reverse and dates from about 120 C.E. By the second century, the coins of the Galilee looked like coins from anywhere else in the Roman empire, but during the time of Jesus they were designed not to offend Jewish sensibilities.

IMPERVIOUS TO IMPURITY. In the miracle at Cana, Jesus turned water into wine. The water was in "six stone jars [of water] for the Jewish rites of purification" (John 2:6). Stone vessels are a telltale sign of a predominantly Jewish population, because, unlike clay vessels, stone vessels are not subject to impurity. First-century C.E. fragments were found in the residential quarter at Sepphoris. Stone vessels such as these are rarely found at sites known to have been inhabited by gentiles but have been found at 23 sites throughout the Galilee. When whole, the stone vessels would have looked like the jars pictured here found in Jerusalem.

YITZHAK MAGEN

as bronze figurines of Pan and Prometheus. Although not entirely absent in first-century Galilee, such depictions are quite rare, presumably because of Jewish prohibitions of representational art.

The same chronological development in visual art can be seen elsewhere in Galilee as well. At the Jewish burial complex at Beth She'arim, where Rabbi Judah ha-Nasi, the revered compiler of the Mishnah (the core of the Talmud) was buried, we find sarcophagi that bear carvings of animals, people and even mythological figures, like Leda and the Swan (Zeus in the form of a swan impregnated Leda).* But all this is from the third and fourth centuries.

Coins aside, only one inscription from the lifetime of Jesus (the first 30 or so years of the first century) has been excavated in Galilee: a market weight from Tiberias with a Greek inscription reading "In the 34th year of Herod the Tetrarch, during the term of office as market overseer of Gaius Julius ..."[9] Few inscriptions date even to later decades of the first century: A Greek inscription of an imperial edict prohibiting tomb robbery probably dates to 44 C.E. or shortly thereafter.[10] Another Greek market weight[11] and a Semitic ostracon (a pottery fragment with writing on it) from Yodefat bear inscriptions too

*See "Beth She'arim: Vast Underground Burial Caves Show Synergism of Greek Art with Jewish Tradition," *Biblical Archaeology Review*, September/October 1992.

fragmentary to reconstruct.[12]

In later centuries, the number of inscriptions vastly increases. Several examples have been found at Sepphoris, including a mid-second-century Greek market weight.[13] Greek inscriptions are also contained in the Dionysus mosaic mentioned earlier. Nearly 280 inscriptions from the late second through the early fourth centuries were found at Beth She'arim (approximately 80 percent in Greek, 16 percent in Hebrew, and the rest in Aramaic or Palmyrene).[14] Latin (and in a few cases, Greek) inscriptions are found on the milestones of Roman roads. The chronological pattern is striking: The later the date, the more likely the inscription is to be in Greek.

Coins with images and inscriptions, however, are an exception to this chronological development. Old Hasmonean coins from as early as the second century B.C.E. were still circulating in the early first century C.E. Some indeed had Semitic inscriptions, but others had Greek inscriptions. Many bore common numismatic images such as cornucopias and plants. Coins struck in pagan cities or by imperial Roman mints naturally had Greek inscriptions and freely depicted living things. A portrait of the Roman emperor was also common on these coins. But until the time of Antipas, no coins were actually struck in Galilee. True, Antipas's coins did contain Greek inscriptions, but this was more a reflection of his desire to conform to the coinage customs of the larger Roman East. In his choice of language, Antipas wanted his coins to blend in, not stand out. He did not, however, depict living things—no gods, animals or portraits of the emperor. Instead, his coins usually depicted a plant, such as a palm tree.

When the cities of Sepphoris and Tiberias struck coins later in the first century, they, too, avoided depictions of living things. Not until the second and third century did Galilean coins portray images of the emperor or deities. A coin struck in Tiberias during Hadrian's reign (second century C.E.), for example, depicted the emperor on one side and Zeus seated in a temple on the other.[15] In this way, Galilee coins became virtually indistinguishable from those elsewhere in the Roman East.

The conclusion is clear: During the early first century C.E., when Jesus lived in Galilee, it was hardly infused with Greco-Roman influence. Instead we should look at it as a region with a cultural climate in flux. It was not totally isolated from the architectural, artistic and linguistic trends of the larger Greco-Roman world, but neither had it fully incorporated them into its own culture. In the time of Jesus, we see what amount to hints of what would come in subsequent centuries.

Another similar and related question arises: What about the people living in the Galilee? Were they Jewish or Greek? The answer is somewhat like the cultural mix: Mostly Jewish, but a few gentiles as well.

This is the situation reflected in the ancient sources that have survived: the Gospels, the histories of Josephus and the writings of the rabbis. They mention *some* gentile Galileans, but few. Josephus, for example, reports that at the outbreak of the First Jewish Revolt against Rome (66–70 C.E.), certain Jews in Tiberias attacked the city's gentile minority.[16] Similarly Matthew 8:5–13 and Luke 7:1–10 mention a gentile centurion (probably an officer in the army of Antipas, rather than a Roman soldier) at Capernaum. But none of the sources gives the impression that gentiles formed an especially significant proportion of Galilee's population.

The archaeological situation confirms this impression. There are three kinds of archaeological indicators that inhabitants of a settlement were Jewish: limestone vessels, ritual baths

RITUAL BATHS such as this first-century *mikveh* found at Gamla, a community in the nearby Golan east of the Galilee, also attest to a Jewish population. Immersion in a *mikveh* removes impurity. *Mikva'ot* have been found at Yodefat, Sepphoris and other sites throughout Jewish Galilee.

SECONDARY BURIAL was common among the Jews at the end of the Second Temple period. About a year after death, when the body had decayed, the bones were reinterred in a bone box called an ossuary. This first-century C.E. limestone ossuary was found in a vaulted mausoleum in the Qiryat Shemu'el section of modern Tiberias. Ossuaries are a clear sign of Jewish habitation.

L.Y. RAHMANI

(*mikva'ot*) and ossuaries.

Most pots and dishes in the ancient world were made of clay. But Jews in Jesus' time also used unusual limestone vessels (also known as chalk vessels).* According to the rabbis, limestone vessels played a special role in the Jewish purity system, because they were believed to be impervious to impurity.[17] Storing liquids in these vessels helped safeguard the contents from becoming ritually unclean. This is illustrated in the famous story in the Gospel of John about the wedding at the Galilean village of Cana: According to John 2:1–11, Jesus and his disciples were guests at the wedding; as the celebration progressed, the hosts ran out of wine. Nearby, however, were "six [empty] stone water jars for the Jewish rites of purification, each holding twenty or thirty gallons." Jesus told the host's

servants to fill the jars with water; when they did so, the water miraculously turned to wine.

Limestone vessels were made in a variety of forms, sometimes carved by hand, sometimes on a lathe and sometimes both ways. They include mugs (often erroneously described as "measuring cups"), bowls and storage jars in various sizes.

Because the use of these stone vessels as Jewish is so well attested in literary sources and since they are rarely found at sites known to have been predominantly gentile, their discovery at a particular site is strong evidence of Jewish habitation. Stone vessels or fragments of such vessels have been found at 23 sites in and near Galilee.

Mikva'ot—plastered, stepped pools carved into bedrock used by Jews as ritual baths to remove impurity—have been discovered in first-century C.E. strata at Sepphoris and Yodefat. Additional *mikva'ot* appear at numerous other Galilean sites between 63 B.C.E. (the beginning of direct Roman rule) and 135 C.E. (the end of the Second, or Bar-Kokhba, Jewish Revolt). A *mikveh* from the first century C.E. was also found at Gamla, a Jewish community east of Galilee.** All this is indicative of Jewish habitation.

The final ethnic indicator comes from Jewish burial practices. Many Jews—but not gentiles—observed a custom called secondary burial. About a year after burial, when the flesh had desiccated, the deceased's bones were gathered up and reburied, usually in an ossuary, a small sarcophagus. Regular readers of *Biblical Archaeology Review* are very familiar with ossuaries because of the controversy generated by the discovery of an ossuary with

CLARA AMIT/ISRAEL ANTIQUITIES AUTHORITY

GODS OF THE PAGAN PANTHEON decorate artifacts of towns surrounding the Galilee. A bulla from the northern village of Kedesh (dating to about 200 B.C.) shows Apollo, the god of archery, with the string of his bow drawn at the ready. However, no pagan artifacts or inscriptions have been found inside Galilee dating to Jesus' time.

*See Yitzhak Magen, "Ancient Israel's Stone Age: Purity in Second Temple Times," *Biblical Archaeology Review*, September/October 1998.

an inscription on it that some scholars have argued refers to James the brother of Jesus.*** Jews began practicing secondary burial in Judea in the late first century B.C.E. These ossuaries are usually made of limestone, though some are made of clay. Exactly when Galilean Jews adopted the practice of second burial is uncertain. There is ample evidence of the practice in Galilee soon after the First Jewish Revolt (66–70 C.E.). It is likely that the custom predates the revolt, however, although the evidence is still somewhat unclear. To be strictly accurate, secondary burial has been attested at a number of Galilean sites in Early Roman (63 B.C.E.–135 C.E.) and later archaeological strata.

What about archaeological evidence for gentiles in Galilee? There simply isn't much, at least during the first century C.E. Inscriptions reflecting the worship of pagan gods are found at the border of Galilee, but not the interior. There are no Galilean statues of gods or goddesses. Figurines of deities are likewise few and far between. Nor have archaeologists found any first-century pagan temples in Galilee, though some point to a structure just across the Galilean border, at et-Tell (possibly Biblical Bethsaida), as a possibility.†

In short, we can conclude that Galilee was predominantly Jewish during Jesus' lifetime. Most of the areas around it, however, were predominantly gentile. For example, pagan Scythopolis

was especially close, as were the pagan cities of Hippos, Caesarea Philippi, and the village of Kedesh in the north. It was on the other side of the Sea of Galilee, the eastern side, for example, that Jesus cured the demoniac(s) by sending the demons into a herd of swine who then ran into the sea and drowned (Matthew 8:28–34; Mark 5:1–20; Luke 8:26–39). The swine would not be seen in a Jewish area.

In Jesus' time, Jewish Galilee had indeed been influenced by some Greco-Roman culture, but only later periods would see that influence flower. And in Jesus' time the Galilee was largely a Jewish enclave. ◼

**As to some of these alleged *mikva'ot*, there is fierce *acacemic* debate. Hanan Eshel, for example, argues that some of the pools at Sepphoris cannot be *mikva'ot* because they do not match later rabbinic descriptions of such baths. In his view, their small size, lack of a partition in the steps leading into the pool, and absence of a storage tank for water suggest that the pools were used for purposes other than removing impurity. Perhaps, he suggests, they were used for regular hygienic bathing. Hanan Eshel, "They're Not Ritual Baths," *Biblical Archeology Review*, July/August 2000. Most scholars note, however, that rabbinic opinions do not yet appear to have been authoritative as early as the first century. They also point out that if such pools were used for regular baths, we would expect to find them at a far greater range of sites, including those that were predominantly gentile. Eric M. Meyers, "Yes, They Are," *Biblical Archeology Review*, July/August 2000; Ronny Reich, "They Are Ritual Baths," *Biblical Archeology Review*, March/April 2002. In my opinion, it is far more likely that these pools are, indeed, *mikva'ot*.

***See André Lemaire, "Burial Box of James the Brother of Jesus," *Biblical Archeology Review*, November/December 2002; Edward J. Keall, Hershel Shanks, "Is It or Isn't It?" *Biblical Archeology Review*, March/April 2003; "'Brother of Jesus' Ossuary—New Tests Bolster Case for Authenticity," *Biblical Archeology Review*, July/August 2003.

†See Rami Arav, Richard A. Freund and John F. Shroder Jr., "Bethsaida Rediscovered," *Biblical Archeology Review*, January/February 2000, which rejects the identification of et-Tell as Bethsaida.

[1]Josephus, *Jewish Antiquities* 16.146–148; *Jewish War* 1.422–425 (Loeb ed.).
[2]See, for example, Mark 6:14–29; Luke 3:1, 23:7–12.
[3]See the sources cited in Mark A. Chancey, *The Myth of a Gentile Galilee*, Society for New Testament Studies Monograph Series 118 (Cambridge: Cambridge Univ. Press, 2002), pp. 69–83.
[4]James F. Strange, "Six Campaigns at Sepphoris: The University of South Florida Excavations, 1983–1989," in Lee I. Levine, ed., *The Galilee in Late Antiquity* (New York and Jerusalem: The Jewish Theological Seminary of America, 1992), pp. 339–356; Carol Meyers and Eric M. Meyers, "Sepphoris," *Oxford Encyclopedia of the Ancient Near East*, vol. 4, (New York and Oxford: Oxford Univ. Press, 1997), pp. 527–536; and Zeev Weiss and Ehud Netzer, "Hellenistic and Roman Sepphoris: The Archaeological Evidence," in Rebecca Martin Nagy, Carol L. Meyers, Eric M. Meyers, and Zeev Weiss, *Sepphoris in Galilee: Crosscurrents of Culture* (Winona Lake, IN: Eisenbrauns, 1996), pp. 29–37.
[5]Josephus, *Jewish War* 2.618 and 3.539–540.
[6]"Roman Stadium Found in Tiberias," *Jerusalem Post*, June 17, 2002.
[7]Vassilios Tzaferis, "A Roman Bath at Rama," *Atiqot* 14 (1980), pp. 66–75.
[8]Carol L. Meyers, Eric M. Meyers, Ehud Netzer and Zeev Weiss, "The Dionysos Mosaic," in Nagy et al., *Sepphoris in Galilee*, pp. 111–116; R. Talgam and Z. Weiss, *The Mosaics of the House of Dionysos at Sepphoris* (Jerusalem: Institute of Archaeology, Hebrew Univ., 2004).
[9]Shraga Qedar, "Two Lead Weights of Herod Antipas and Agrippa II and the Early History of Tiberias," *Israel Numismatic Journal* 9 (1986–1987), pp. 29–35.
[10]Eric M. Meyers and James F. Strange, *Archaeology, the Rabbis, and Early Christianity* (Nashville: Abingdon, 1981), pp. 83–84.
[11]Qedar, "Two Lead Weights of Herod Antipas and Agrippa II and the Early History of Tiberias," pp. 29–35.
[12]David Adan-Bayewitz and Mordechai Aviam, "Iotapata, Josephus, and the Siege of 67: Preliminary Report on the 1992–1994 Seasons," *Journal of Roman Archaeology* 10 (1997), pp. 131–165, esp. p. 152.
[13]See comments by Meshorer in Nagy et al., *Sepphoris in Galilee*, p. 201.
[14]The statistics are from Lee I. Levine, "Beth She'arim," *Oxford Encyclopedia of Archaeology of the Near East*, vol. 2, pp. 309–311.
[15]Yaakov Meshorer, *City—Coins of Eretz—Israel and the Decapolis in the Roman Period* (Jerusalem: Israel Museum, 1985), p. 34.
[16]Josephus, *Life* 65–67.
[17]*Mishnah Kelim* 10.1; *Mishnah Oholoth* 5.5; *Mishnah Yadayim* 1.2.

FEW PLACES BETTER ILLUSTRATE the layered history that archaeology uncovers than the little ridge known as the City of David, the oldest inhabited part of Jerusalem. For example, to tell the story of the Pool of Siloam, where Jesus cured the blind man, we must go back 700 years before that—to the time of the Assyrian monarch Sennacherib and his siege of Jerusalem.

Hezekiah, the Judahite king at that time, could see the Assyrian siege coming. Protective steps were clearly called for, especially to protect Jerusalem's water supply. The only source of fresh water at this time was the Gihon Spring, near the floor of the adjacent Kidron Valley. So Hezekiah decided on a major engineering project—he would construct a tunnel under the ridge on which the City of David lay to bring the water of the spring to the other, less vulnerable, side of Jerusalem. It was dug by two teams of tunnelers working from opposite ends, meeting in the middle—it's still a mystery how they managed to meet, but they did. A memorial plaque was carved in the tunnel wall to commemorate the feat—the famous Siloam Inscription, now in the Istanbul Museum (it was discovered in Ottoman times). Water flowed through the tunnel from the spring to the Pool of Siloam at the other end. It is still known as Hezekiah's Tunnel, and it is still a thrill for tourists to walk through its 1750-foot length.

Where Jesus
Cured the Blind Man

HERSHEL SHANKS

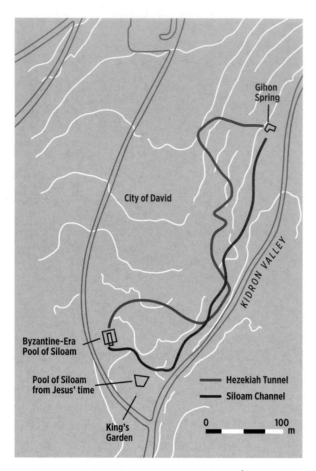

Gihon
Spring

City of David

KIDRON VALLEY

Byzantine-Era
Pool of Siloam

Pool of Siloam
from Jesus' time

King's
Garden

—— Hezekiah Tunnel
—— Siloam Channel

0   100
         m

WHILE WATCHING MUNICIPAL WORKERS replace a sewer pipe in the City of David, south of Jerusalem's Temple Mount, archaeologist Eli Shukron noticed that the construction equipment had revealed two ancient steps. previous pages) Shukron quickly notified his colleague Ronny Reich, who identified the steps as part of the Pool of Siloam from the late Second Temple Period (first century B.C.-first century A.D.), as further excavations soon confirmed. It was at the Pool of Siloam, according to the Gospel of John, that Jesus cured the blind man (John 9:1-11). The newly discovered pool is adjacent to an area referred to as the King's Garden and is just southeast of what had long been called the Pool of Siloam (see plan above). The other pool, however, does not date to Jesus' time but to the fourth century (a photo of this later Pool of Siloam appears on p. 52).

The waters of Siloam are mentioned by the prophet Isaiah, a contemporary of Hezekiah's, who refers to "the gently flowing waters of Siloam" (Shiloah in Hebrew) (Isaiah 8:6). When the exiles returned from Babylon and rebuilt the walls of Jerusalem, Nehemiah tells us that a certain Shallun rebuilt "the wall of the Pool of Shiloah by the King's Garden" (Nehemiah 3:15).

In Jesus' time the Pool of Siloam figures in the cure of a man who had been blind from birth.

Jesus spits on the ground and mixes his saliva with the mud, which he smears on the blind man's eyes. He then tells the man "to wash in the Pool of Siloam." When the blind man does so, he is able to see (John 9:1-7).

We still haven't found the Pool of Siloam from Isaiah's and Hezekiah's time. We're not even sure where it was. The same is true regarding the pool in Nehemiah's time. In the Byzantine period the empress Eudocia (c. 400-460) built a church and a pool where the water debouches from Hezekiah's Tunnel to commemorate the miracle of the blind man. Early in the last century archaeologists found the remains of that church, over which today sits a mosque. The church and the pool are mentioned in several Byzantine pilgrim itineraries. Until last year, it was this pool that people meant when they talked of the Pool of Siloam.

Now we have found an earlier pool, the pool as it existed in Jesus' time—and it is a much grander affair.

As with so much in archaeology, it was stumbled on, not part of a planned excavation. In June 2004 archaeologists Ronny Reich and Eli Shukron were digging in the area of the Gihon Spring where Hezekiah's Tunnel begins. Far to the south, between the end of the rock ridge that forms the City of David and a lush green orchard that is often identified as the Biblical King's Garden, is a narrow alley through which a sewer pipe runs carrying waste from the valley west of the City of David into the Kidron Valley east of the City of David. The city authorities needed to repair or replace this sewer and sent workers with heavy equipment to do some excavating. Eli was watching the operation, when suddenly he saw two steps appear. He immediately halted the work and called Ronny, who came rushing down. As soon as Ronny saw the steps, he exclaimed, "These must be steps going down to the Pool of Siloam during the Second Temple Period." He took a few pictures and wrote a report to Jon Seligman, the district archaeologist for Jerusalem. A quick response was called for because the winter rains were fast approaching and the sewer pipe had to be repaired or replaced. Ronny and Eli were quickly authorized to excavate the area on behalf of the Israeli Antiquities Authority. The more they excavated, the more steps they found, and the wider the steps became.

They have now excavated the entire length of

HERSHEL SHANKS

THREE SETS OF STAIRS (above), each with five steps, have been uncovered at the New Testament-era Pool of Siloam. The excavators have exposed an area 225 feet long on one side of the pool and have reached both corners of that side (one corner is shown at right). The corners are somewhat greater than 90 degrees, indicating that the pool was not a square but a trapezoid.

the steps on the side adjacent to the rock ridge of the City of David. There are in fact three short segments of descending stairways of five steps each. The first leads down to a narrow landing. The second leads to another landing and the third leads down to the final level (so far). The size of the pool itself would vary, depending on the level of the water. When it was full, it probably covered all of the steps. The landings served as a kind of esplanade for people to stand on when the steps were submerged in water.

The archaeologists also uncovered the two stepped corners at either end of these steps. So we know how wide the pool was at this point: more than 225 feet. We also know that the steps existed on at least three sides of the pool.

HERSHEL SHANKS

RONNY REICH WAS the first to identify the steps as part of the Pool of Siloam from the time of Jesus. Now the leading archaeologist specializing in Jerusalem, Reich worked with the late Nahman Avigad in the Old City's Jewish Quarter and has also dug at the western wall of the Temple Mount. His excavations at the Gihon Spring have revolutionized our understanding of the city's ancient water supply system.

The corners are not exactly at right angles, however; they are a little more than 90 degrees. The pool appears to have been a trapezoid, widening apron-like as it descends into the valley. How far into the valley the pool extended, the archaeologists are not sure. Ronny's best guess is that it is about the same as the width of the pool on the side they have uncovered.

Many times archaeologists are unsure of the date of what they find. But in this case, there is no question. Ideally, archaeologists want two dates: the date of construction and the date when the facility went out of use. Here the archaeologists are fortunate to have both.

The pool had two phases. The stone steps are part of the second phase. Under the stone steps and in places where the stones are missing, the excavators were able see that in the first phase the steps were plastered. Only in the second phase were the steps faced with stones. The excavators went over the early steps with a metal detector, and in four places it beeped, revealing four coins *in the plaster*. These coins would date the first phase of the pool.

They were all coins of Alexander Jannaeus (103-76 B.C.), one of the later Hasmonean (Jewish) kings who were succeeded in 37 B.C. by

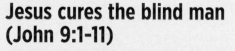

Jesus cures the blind man (John 9:1-11)

As he walked along, he saw a man blind from birth. [2]His disciples asked him, "Rabbi, who sinned, this man or his parents, that he was born blind?" [3]Jesus answered, "Neither this man nor his parents sinned, he was born blind so that God's works might be revealed in him. [4]We must work the works of him who sent me while it is day; night is coming when no one can work. [5]As long as I am in the world, I am the light of the world." [6]When he had said this, he spat on the ground and made mud with the saliva, and spread the mud on the man's eyes, [7]saying to him, "Go, wash in the pool of Siloam" (which means Sent). Then he went and washed and came back able to see. [8]The neighbors and those who had seen him before as a beggar began to ask, "Is this not the man who used to sit and beg?" [9]Some were saying "It is he." Others were saying, "No, but it is someone like him." He kept saying, "I am the man." [10]But they kept asking him, "Then how were your eyes opened?" [11]He answered, "The man called Jesus made mud, spread it on my eyes, and said to me, 'Go to Siloam and wash.' Then I went and washed and received my sight."

Herod the Great. The excavators cannot be sure precisely how long these coins were in circulation before being embedded in the plaster of the first phase of the Pool of Siloam. But they can say with some assurance that the pool was constructed in the late Hasmonean period or early Herodian period. They may know more precisely if they dig under the steps and find a coin from Herod's time. Then the pool would be Herodian.

We also know from coins how long the pool was in use. Near one corner of the pool they excavated part of a plaza or terrace and found nothing but late Second Temple pottery (which ended with the Roman destruction of Jerusalem in 70 A.D.). Most significantly, they found a dozen coins from the period of the First Jewish Revolt against Rome. The revolt lasted from 66 to 70 A.D. The excavated coins date from years 2, 3 and 4 of the revolt. The pool was therefore used until the end of the revolt, after which it was abandoned.

This area, the lowest spot in all Jerusalem, was not inhabited again until the Byzantine period. Every year the winter rains flowing down the valley deposited another layer of mud in the pool. And after the Roman destruction of the city, the pool was no longer cleaned. Over the centuries a thick layer of mud accumulated and the pool gradually disappeared. The archaeologists found it under nearly 10 feet of mud in places.

THE SILOAM POOL as it might have looked during the New Testament era is shown here in an artist's rendition. Bathers would have enjoyed a view of the Kidron Valley, just east of the City of David. In the Gospel of John, when Jesus cures the blind man, he tells him, "Go to Siloam and wash" (John 9:11). The pool probably served as a *miqveh*, a Jewish ritual bath.

When Byzantine Christians returned to the area in the fourth century, they assumed the Pool of Siloam referred to in the New Testament was at the end of Hezekiah's Tunnel, so they built their pool and a commemorative church where the tunnel comes out of the rock. This pool figures in numerous 19th-century engravings. As late as the 1970s, Arab women still washed clothes in this pool. It is well worth a visit.

What function the Pool of Siloam served in Jesus' time is not entirely clear. Undoubtedly, thousands of pilgrims would come to Jerusalem on the three Biblically ordained pilgrim festivals—Passover, Weeks (Pentecost, or Shavuoth) and Tabernacles (Succoth). They may well have camped in the adjacent Kidron Valley and been supplied with drinking and cooking water from the pool. The water in the pool would also qualify as a *miqveh*, for ritual bathing, points out Reich, who is a leading expert on *mikva'ot*. Indeed its naturally flowing spring water was of the highest level of sanctity. The water in a *miqveh* is usually standing

HERSHEL SHANKS

A WOMAN KNEELS to do her laundry (photo at left) in what had long been known as the Pool of Siloam. Byzantine-era Christians assumed this pool was the Biblical Siloam and built a church here; this pool was a popular destination for pilgrims and was the subject of a 19th-century illustration by W.H. Bartlett (below). Thanks to the recent discovery, we now know that the Biblical Pool of Siloam was just southeast of this site.

How Historical Is the Gospel of John?

The Gospels, the first four books of the New Testament, tell the story of the life of Jesus. Yet only one—the Gospel of John—claims to be an eyewitness account, the testimony of the unnamed "disciple whom Jesus loved." ("This is the disciple who is testifying to these things and wrote these things, and we know that his testimony is true" [John 21:24]). Matthew, Mark and Luke are so alike in their telling that they are called the Synoptic Gospels, meaning, "seen together"—the parallels are clear when they are looked at side by side. Matthew and Luke follow the version of events in Mark, which is thought by scholars to be the earliest and most historically accurate Gospel. John, however, does not include the same incidents or chronology found in the other three Gospels, and the fact that it is so different has spurred a debate over whether John's Gospel is historical or not.*

Several hypotheses have attempted to explain why so much of Jesus' life not portrayed in the Synoptics is present in John and vice versa. One hypothesis claims that John recorded many of the events that occurred before the arrest of

*For more on the question of John's historical reliability, see D. Moody Smith, "John: Historian or Theologian?" *Bible Review,* October 2004.

John the Baptist, while the Synoptics all have Jesus' ministry beginning only after the arrest. Another holds that John was written last, by someone who knew about the other three Gospels but who wished to write a spiritual gospel instead of an historical one. There is also the possibility that the author of John did not know of Mark and hence did not have the same information.

One of the facts in dispute among the four Gospels is the length of Jesus' ministry. According to the Synoptics, it lasted only about a year, while John has Jesus ministering between two and three years. The Jesus of John's telling also knew Jerusalem well and had traveled there three or four times. The Synoptics, however, have Jesus visit Jerusalem only once. In John, Jesus had friends near Jerusalem, including Mary, Martha and Lazarus of the town of Bethany, which is just outside of the city on the east slope of the Mount of Olives.

The author of John also knew Jerusalem well, as is evident from the geographic and place name information throughout the book. He mentions, among others, the Sheep Gate Pool (Bethesda), the Siloam Pool and Jacob's Well. The geographic specificity lends credence to John's account.

Another aspect of John that may be more historically accurate than

the Synoptics is the account of the crucifixion and the events that led up to it. The Synoptics say that Jesus' Last Supper was the Passover meal—held that year on a Thursday evening (Jewish holidays begin at sunset)—and they would have us believe that the Sanhedrin, the high court, gathered at the beginning of a major holiday to interrogate Jesus and hand him over to the Romans. John, in contrast, has Jesus handed over for crucifixion on "the day of Preparation of Passover week, about the sixth hour." According to John, the Last Supper is not a Passover meal (because the holiday that year did not start until Friday evening), and Jesus is crucified and buried before Passover begins. In John's account Jesus becomes the Passover sacrificial lamb, which was offered the afternoon before the Passover holiday. Some scholars suggest that John may be more historical regarding the crucifixion than the other three Gospels.

Given John's familiarity with Jerusalem and its environs, it is very possible that he had visited the Pool of Siloam, which he mentions in connection with the story of the curing of the blind man (a story that appears only in John's Gospel). It is that pool that has only recently been uncovered, as described in the accompanying article.

water, even though it is required to flow into the pool naturally. But here the spring flowed continuously, refreshing the water. However, ritual bathing in a *miqveh* must be in the nude. Perhaps there was some means of providing privacy.

Whether the Pool of Siloam in Hezekiah and Isaiah's time was located in the same place as in Jesus' time remains a question. Even if it was in the same spot, it may have been a different size. Ronny and Eli would like to make a cut under the steps, which would give some indication of an earlier pool. If they find Iron Age pottery (tenth-sixth century B.C.), they can conclude that the Pool of Siloam

from Hezekiah's and Isaiah's time was in this same location. However, Ronny and Eli do not want to dig into the verdant orchard that now fills the unexcavated portion of the New Testament-era Pool of Siloam. Besides, it belongs to the Greek Orthodox Church, which, like Ronny and Eli, would not want the orchard destroyed. But they would like to make a very small cut through the trees to see how deep the pool is and to learn whether there are Iron Age remains beneath. Perhaps the church, appreciating the significance of this place, will permit this. The church's orchard suddenly has great significance for the history of its faith.

THE GOSPEL OF THOMAS

Jesus Said What?

SIMON GATHERCOLE

JESUS SAID, "BLESSED IS THE LION which the man eats, and the lion becomes man."

Jesus said, "Be passers-by!"

Jesus said, "For every woman who makes herself male will enter the kingdom of heaven."

This hardly sounds like the Jesus familiar to us from the New Testament. It is from the *Gospel of Thomas*, one of the earliest remakings of Jesus after the four canonical gospels. This gospel must have seemed to some ancient readers, as it does even to scholars today, as "a riddle wrapped in a mystery inside an enigma," as Winston Churchill once said of Russia. The strange world of the *Gospel of Thomas* is of interest not so much because one can find authentic traditions from or about Jesus in it—it doesn't have any real claim to historical veracity—but because it provides a fascinating window into some of the controversies in the Christian community around the middle of the second century C.E. when it was written.

We have known about the *Gospel of Thomas* for a long time. A number of Church Fathers mention it disparagingly, from as far back as Hippolytus and Origen in the third century C.E. In his *Refutation of All the Heresies*, Hippolytus includes it in a list of writings used by Gnostics. Origen includes it in a list of false gospels that tried to write down the truth about Jesus but failed.

THE PROOF IS IN THE PAPYRUS. The discovery of a complete Coptic text of the *Gospel of Thomas* among the Nag Hammadi codices proved that the three Greek leaves found 200 miles to the north and 50 years earlier were indeed from the *Gospel of Thomas*.

BODLEIAN LIBRARY, UNIVERSITY OF OXFORD

HOUGHTON LIBRARY, HARVARD UNIVERSITY

"SAYINGS OF JESUS" (the *Logia*) is what A.S. Hunt and B.P. Grenfell called the papyrus when they published it in 1897 after its discovery during their first excavation season at Oxyrhynchus, Egypt. Now referred to as POxy1, both sides of the early- to mid-third-century leaf are written in Greek. Was this a fragment of the *Gospel of Thomas* referred to by the Church Fathers? The answer would come only half a century later.

But don't confuse the *Gospel of Thomas* with the *Infancy Gospel of Thomas*, as scholars did until quite recently. Until the 20th century, most Christian writers down the ages, as well as early critical scholars, assumed that the *Gospel of Thomas* mentioned by the Church Fathers was actually a different work, what we now call the *Infancy Gospel of Thomas*. The *Infancy Gospel of Thomas* is a narrative account of periods in Jesus' childhood, including legendary episodes in which Jesus strikes dead another boy who bumps into him, miraculously lengthens a wooden beam to help his stepfather, Joseph, with his carpentry, raises from the dead his friend who falls off a roof on which they were playing, and makes live sparrows out of clay. This *Infancy Gospel of Thomas* was probably written at roughly the same time as the *Gospel of Thomas*, but the name Thomas only got attached to the

JESUS TO THOMAS. A badly preserved papyrus fragment from Oxyrhynchus contained sayings of Jesus reputed to have been dictated to his apostle Thomas. Together with two other fragments, this seemed to confirm that this was from the heretofore lost *Gospel of Thomas*.

Infancy Gospel centuries later. The "real" *Gospel of Thomas* (though it is certainly not written by the apostle Thomas) is actually a collection of 114 dialogues and sayings in which Jesus utters statements like those at the beginning of this article.

From the references I've mentioned by Church Fathers, we've known the title of the *Gospel of Thomas* for centuries, but the *contents* have only come to light quite recently. The first discoveries of the contents of the *Gospel of Thomas* came in the first season of digging in the ancient rubbish

dump of Oxyrhynchus in Egypt—the place from which we get so many of the earliest fragments of Biblical and classical literature, as well as a host of everyday bills and letters.* To the amazement of the Oxford scholars A.S. Hunt and B.P. Grenfell, who took part in the dig and published the texts unearthed, a Greek fragment of what they called the *Logia* (or "Sayings of Jesus") was discovered in the very first season and published in 1897. To their further amazement, the second season (in 1903) yielded another Greek fragment, this one making the claim that the sayings in it were dictated by Jesus to his disciple Thomas. Scholars then began to suspect that this might be a "Gospel of Thomas." Another Greek fragment, very badly damaged, was published in 1904. These three fragments, labeled by scholars Oxyrhynchus Papyri 1, 654 and 655, are now housed respectively in Oxford University, the British Library in London and Harvard University. According to scholars who have analyzed the handwriting, these manuscripts date from around the beginning of the third century to the middle of that century. (There has not been a detailed paleographical study of the handwriting of these

*Stephen J. Patterson, "The Oxyrhynchus Papyri—The Remarkable Discovery You've Probably Never Heard Of," *Biblical Archaeology Review*, March/April 2011; Amanda Kolson Hurley, "Priceless Garbage—The Papyri of Oxyrhynchus," Sidebar to "Literacy in the Time of Jesus," *Biblical Archaeology Review*, July/August 2003.

HERO OF THE NAG HAMMADI CODICES? An Egyptian peasant named Mohammed Ali claimed to have unearthed the sealed jar containing Coptic texts while digging for fertilizer near a cliff 7 miles northeast of Nag Hammadi in late 1945 or early 1946. He says he shattered the jar and discovered the mid-fourth-century manuscripts inside. Doubts have arisen, however.

fragments for a long time; this needs to be done.) So at about the same time that Hippolytus and Origen were making disparaging remarks about the *Gospel of Thomas*, others were making the copies of it that we now have from Oxyrhynchus.

Even with the discoveries of these three fragments, it wasn't certain that they belonged to the *Gospel of Thomas*. But in 1945 or 1946, the Nag Hammadi codices were discovered, and in one of them was a complete translation of the *Gospel of Thomas* in Coptic!

It is an ingrained part of the mythology of scholarship on Gnosticism and the Nag Hammadi codices that an Egyptian peasant named Mohammed Ali discovered the Nag Hammadi codices in a jar while he was digging for *sabakh*, a kind of fertilizer, shortly after the end of the Second World War. In the official account, the find-spot was by a cliff called Jabal al-Tarif, around 7 miles northeast of Nag Hammadi in Upper (i.e., southern) Egypt.[1] The story is told, for example, in Elaine Pagels's best-selling *The Gnostic Gospels*.[2] The find is commonly dated to early January

1946. According to some accounts, the discoverers remember that it was around the time of Coptic Christmas (January 7). It was then that Mohammed Ali and his brothers avenged the killing of their father, then cut out the heart of their father's murderer and each ate a share.

Large parts—and perhaps the whole—of the story are mythology. Different tellings of the story have yielded different results: Mark Goodacre of Duke University notes that the height of the jar in question can range from 2 feet to 6 feet![3] Nicola Denzey Lewis and Justine Ariel Blount comment that finding the jar when digging for fertilizer in that area is hard to imagine, given that papyrus would be unlikely to survive for centuries of inundations of the Nile![4]

Whatever the truth about the discovery, however, there has never been any doubt about the authenticity and antiquity of the Nag Hammadi codices, wherever they may have been found.

In what became known as the second of the Nag Hammadi codices, *Thomas* appeared in full (in Coptic)—sandwiched between a Gnostic work, the *Apocryphon of John*, and another apocryphal gospel, the *Gospel of Philip*. The Nag Hammadi text of the *Gospel of Thomas* at last proved that the three Greek fragments from Oxyrhynchus are indeed from the *Gospel of Thomas*. From the Nag Hammadi codices, the world now has access to the full database of the *Gospel of Thomas*'s 114 sayings of Jesus.

Could these sayings shed new light on who Jesus was? Because of the enormous importance of this question, scholars began to investigate how close in time the *Gospel of Thomas* was to Jesus' life on earth. Could the book be as early as—or maybe even earlier than—the New Testament Gospels? This question of when *Thomas* was written is intertwined with the questions of who originally wrote it and in what language (certainly not the Coptic of the Nag Hammadi Codex). Was it an early Aramaic gospel from the generation after Jesus' ministry? Or was it—at least at its

core—a product of Syriac Christianity around 200 C.E.? We already find suggestions close to these two extremes in the early church. Some may have thought it was really written by the disciple Thomas. On the other hand, Church Fathers who (rightly) could not believe that the apostle Thomas really wrote this gospel thought that it must have been written by a member of the Manichaean sect, because Mani had a disciple called Thomas. But Mani's ministry did not begin until the mid-to-late third century, and so this would put the *Gospel of Thomas* into a time frame of about 275 C.E. at the earliest. This is impossible, however, because, as we have seen, the *Gospel of Thomas* was already known around 200–250 C.E. both among the Oxyrhynchus papyri and from references in early Church Fathers. In modern scholarship, some of the same arguments for *Thomas* having early Aramaic features are also used as evidence for *Thomas* being a much later *Syriac* production. (Syriac is a dialect of Aramaic; early in the history of Syriac the two might be hard to distinguish.) In fact, these apparently Semitic features of the language that we can see in our Coptic manuscript of *Thomas* from Nag Hammadi as well as in the Greek fragments from Oxyrhynchus are fairly unremarkable and often just a matter of "Biblical idiom." *Thomas* was almost certainly written in Greek sometime around the middle of the second century.[5]

What sort of vision of Christianity does the *Gospel of Thomas* propound? Is it "Gnostic," as often supposed, or is it more likely just a mildly quirky variation on the orthodox theme? Again, neither of these supposed extremes work.

Of course, any discussion of whether or not a work is "Gnostic" depends on one's view of Gnosticism, which includes the question of whether such a thing as Gnosticism even existed. The best recent scholarship on this topic, though, has seen that the Gnostics were actually an identifiable group in antiquity. We can deduce this from the fact that both early Church Fathers (like Irenaeus and Hippolytus) and pagan Platonist philosophers (like Porphyry) independently name a particular group "the Gnostics." And both the Church Fathers and the Platonists also described the Gnostics as believing specifically that both the creator god of the world and the world itself are evil.[6] This was a view that Christian and pagan critics alike thought outrageous!

Those who have thought that *Thomas* is Gnostic have seized upon the negative views of the body and the world evident in the book. And it is certainly true that the body and the world are seen in a negative light in *Thomas*. For example, in talking about the fact that the soul or spirit has come into the body, Jesus says: "I do marvel at how this great wealth has come to dwell in this poverty!" (*Gospel of Thomas* 28.3). The opposition of "wealth" and "poverty" shows up the sharp contrast between the precious soul and the worthless body. Jesus is similarly negative about the material cosmos: "Whoever has come to know the world has found a corpse" (*Gospel of Thomas* 56.1). In *Thomas*, to be dead like a corpse is to be in the realm of ultimate perdition; to be classed as "dead" is about as bad an insult as can be hurled.

Nevertheless, it has always been something of an embarrassment for the "Gnostic" view of *Thomas* that there is no talk of an evil demiurge, a creation that is intrinsically evil, or of other familiar themes such as "aeons" (a technical term for the divine realms in the heavens). Properly Gnostic gospels such as the *Gospel of Judas*, and the Nag Hammadi *Gospel of the Egyptians*, have very complicated accounts of how multitudes of deities and aeons come into existence from a demonic power before the birth of the world. There is nothing of this in *Thomas*, though.

But neither does it work to see *Thomas* as simply a stone's throw from the kind of Christianity or Christianities evident in the New Testament and in "apostolic fathers" such as Clement of Rome, Ignatius and Polycarp.

One of the most striking features of *Thomas* is that it condemns prayer, along with other traditional practices: "If you fast, you will give birth to sin in yourselves. And if you pray, you will be condemned. And if you give alms, you will do ill to your spirits" (*Gospel of Thomas* 14.1–3). We will come back to this condemnation of prayer in a moment.

"THE GOSPEL ACCORDING TO THOMAS" appears in larger letters and indented at the end of a complete Coptic translation of 114 sayings of Jesus found near Nag Hammadi. In this period it was more common to write titles at the end than at the beginning. The Nag Hammadi Library now resides at the Coptic Museum in Cairo, Egypt.

Similarly, Old Testament Scripture is given short shrift in another saying:

His disciples said to him, "Twenty-four prophets[7] spoke in Israel. And did all of them speak about you?"

He said to them, "You have neglected the living one in front of you, and spoken of the dead" (*Gospel of Thomas* 52.1–2).

Here the disciples seem to reflect a traditional Christian view of Jesus' fulfillment of Scripture, the same view we see in the canonical Gospels (e.g., in Matthew 5:17–20; Mark 9:12–13; Luke 24:25–27, 44–47; John 5:39). But Jesus' answer to the disciples' question is a surprise: He denies any connection between himself and Scripture and dismisses the Biblical authors or prophets as simply "dead." As with the world being a corpse, as already mentioned, this is not just a comment on their mortality; rather, in *Thomas*, "death" is a state of complete spiritual doom. The *Gospel of Thomas* portrays a Jesus and a body of teaching cut off from their Jewish origins. This distance

PAYING YOUR WAY. In the *Gospel of Thomas*, getting to a higher spiritual realm after death involved knowing the right answers to demonic interrogation. In other cultures, getting there involved a payment to a kind of gatekeeper. This first-century C.E. coin found at Jericho in the mouth of a skull was thought to be used as "fare" to allow passage to the afterlife. The date is the sixth year of Herod Agrippa's reign. It features three ears of barley on the reverse.

from Judaism can be seen in *Gospel of Thomas* 53, where Jesus dismisses the practice of circumcision as unnatural.

We can return now to the theme of prayer. *Thomas*'s rejection of it is not just an antitraditional gesture, but rather gives an interesting clue to the theology of the book, in particular *Thomas*'s understanding of the "kingdom of God." In the canonical Gospels, the "kingdom of God" is his reign; God remakes this world in conformity with his own plan—hence, the Lord's Prayer: "Your kingdom come, your will be done, on earth as it is in heaven" (Matthew 6:10; cf. Luke 11:2). God's kingdom is his perfect will, coming to pass here specifically in the Gospels through Jesus' reign as God's messianic king. It is very much something that comes from outside, from God himself, to human beings through Jesus' ministry.

In the *Gospel of Thomas*, however, the picture is quite different: The kingdom is *something that indwells in elect disciples, a kind of "true soul."* In some ways, it can be regarded as a fragment of Jesus himself, or at least of the divine. We can see, therefore, why prayer is not just dispensable, but actually illegitimate: Prayer is an appeal to a transcendent God outside of oneself; for a Thomasine disciple to pray would be to deny that one is intrinsically indwelt by the divine.

Some of the details are vague, because the *Gospel of Thomas* is a collection of often enigmatic sayings, but it is tolerably clear that this *true soul* is what needs to escape from this woeful world and from the physical body which binds the soul in the present. This is necessary because the body and the world are heading for death, and the whole purpose of the *Gospel of Thomas* is to provide the means to immortality. The first saying of Jesus in *Thomas* is "Whoever finds the interpretation of these sayings will not taste death." Words for "knowing" or "understanding" (*sooun, eime, gnōsis*) appear 32 times in the *Gospel of Thomas*, which is an extraordinarily dense concentration when one considers that *Thomas* is much shorter than the New Testament Gospels; *Thomas* is roughly the length of Mark 1–6.

Finding true understanding and knowledge is of vital importance in *Thomas*: This knowledge comes exclusively through revelation from Jesus; "I will give you what eye has not seen, and what ear has not heard, and what hand has not touched, nor has it ascended to the heart of man" (*Gospel of Thomas* 17). A key aspect of this knowledge involves training the soul to regard this world and all its vanities as insignificant. Hence, although a number of worldly institutions are not necessarily condemned as evil, they are regarded as matters of complete indifference. These include money (*Gospel of Thomas* 95; 100), clothes (36), diet (14) and family (55; 99).

Knowing how to navigate one's way through demonic interrogation as one ascends to the higher spiritual realms after death (and perhaps in mystical experiences during the present life as well) is vital—rather like going through customs and border control, where one has to present a passport and say the right words. Some ancients thought it necessary to pay the ferryman Charon to take the dead across the rivers Styx and Acheron to Hades. In Egypt it was thought that the "Books of the Dead" would equip the dead person with the necessary spells to pass the respective doorkeepers to the afterlife. A huge number of scrolls of the Books of the Dead have survived. Archaeologists have also discovered skeletons with coins in their mouths, in line with the myth of Charon.* In *Thomas*, the interrogation goes as follows:

If they say to you, "From where have you come?"

say to them, "We have come from the light, where the light came into being all of its own accord and stood and appeared in their images."

If they say to you, "Is it you?" (i.e., "Who are you?")

say, "We are its children and we are the elect of the living Father."

If they ask you, "What is the sign of your Father in you?"

say to them, "It is motion and rest."

(*Gospel of Thomas* 50.1–3)

Thus, it is critical to say the right thing about one's identity and origins (as is common in both Egyptian mythology and Valentinian and Gnostic writings), as well as having the right "sign," namely the enigmatic "motion and rest." The combination, then, of a rigorous attitude toward worldly institutions, an exclusive focus on Jesus' revelation, and a knowledge of how to attain union with the divine by crossing the perilous, demon-infested limbo, is key to the soul's escape from this miserable world.

Having the complete text of the *Gospel of Thomas*—even if only in a Coptic translation—affords us a fascinating insight into the diverse views about Jesus and salvation in the early decades of Christianity. Debates about key issues such as which texts gave the authoritative picture of Jesus, what status the Old Testament and traditional Jewish practices should have in the church, what the relationship is between the soul and the body, what attitudes should be taken to money and family—these debates and many others are reflected in the *Gospel of Thomas*. In the midst of these controversies that characterized early Christianity, *Thomas* proposes a radical vision of an un-Jewish Jesus and of a rejection of the world and the body in favor of a focus on rigorous training of the soul to enable its escape to re-enter the divine. In these 114 short sayings, the compiler of the *Gospel of Thomas* insists that it is his gospel that at last provides the key to knowledge. 🔲

---

*Gabriel Barkay, "The Riches of Ketef Hinnom," *Biblical Archaeology Review*, July/August/September/October 2009; Zvi Greenhut, "Burial Cave of the Caiaphas Family," *Biblical Archaeology Review*, September/October 1992; Rachel Hachlili, "Ancient Burial Customs Preserved in Jericho Hills," *Biblical Archaeology Review*, July/August 1979.

[1] James M. Robinson, "The Discovery of the Nag Hammadi Codices," *Biblical Archaeologist* 42 (1979), pp. 206–224, esp. p. 209.

[2] Elaine Pagels, *The Gnostic Gospels* (New York: Random House, 1979), pp. xiii–xiv.

[3] Mark Goodacre, "How Reliable Is the Story of the Nag Hammadi Discovery?" *Journal for the Study of the New Testament* 35 (2013), pp. 303–322, esp. pp. 305–306.

[4] Nicola Denzey Lewis & Justine Ariel Blount, "Rethinking the Origins of the Nag Hammadi Codices," *Journal of Biblical Literature* 133 (2014), pp. 399–419, esp. p. 402.

[5] Simon J. Gathercole, *The Composition of the Gospel of Thomas: Original Language and Influences* (Cambridge: Cambridge Univ. Press, 2012). This helps account for various factors. First, *Thomas* shows that it has been influenced by Luke's Gospel in particular, and also Matthew. (In fact, it probably refers to the disciple Matthew because he was known as a gospel writer.) Second, it is also influenced by some epistles of Paul, notably Romans but perhaps also 1 Corinthians. Third, there is an intriguing fragmentary statement in which Jesus says, "I will destroy this house, and no one will be able to build it [...]" (*Gospel of Thomas* 71). Most scholars take this as a prediction that the Temple will be destroyed, and that it will never be rebuilt. Some have taken this to be the kind of saying that would have come into existence soon after 70 C.E. when the Romans destroyed the Temple. However, *Thomas*'s confidence about the non-rebuilding of the Temple would be unlikely to follow directly from the events of the First Jewish Revolt. For a generation or so after 70 C.E., one could not necessarily assume that the Temple would never be rebuilt. Josephus, for example, wrote that many disasters had befallen the Jews, but that each time their fortunes had been restored; even with the Temple, however many times it may be destroyed, it will inevitably be rebuilt: "The God who made you will give back to your citizens both cities and the Temple, and the loss of these things will not happen just once, but many times" (*Antiquities of the Jews* 4.314). It was only after the Bar Kochba revolt in 132–135 C.E. that the rebuilding of the Temple began to look next to impossible. And this is the time when other Christian theologians, such as Justin Martyr, Aristo of Pella, Tertullian and Origen, began to see the destruction of the Temple as the fulfillment of Old Testament prophecy, and as a permanent desolation. The combined evidence of factors such as *Thomas*'s literary influences, as well as his view of the Temple, has led scholars like Mark Goodacre and myself to view *Thomas* as a product of sometime in the mid-second century. In addition to my book already mentioned, see further Mark Goodacre, *Thomas and the Gospels: The Case for Thomas's Familiarity with the Synoptics* (Grand Rapids: Eerdmans, 2012); Simon Gathercole, *The Gospel of Thomas: Introduction and Commentary* (Leiden: Brill, 2014).

[6] See, for example, Mark J. Edwards, "Gnostics and Valentinians in the Church Fathers," *Journal of Theological Studies* (*JTS*) 40 (1989), pp. 26–47; Mark J. Edwards, "Neglected Texts in the Study of Gnosticism," *JTS* 41 (1990), pp. 26–50; Bentley Layton, "Prolegomena to the Study of Gnosticism," in L.M. White & O.L. Yarbrough, eds., *The Social World of the First Christians: Essays in Honor of Wayne Meeks* (Minneapolis: Augsburg Fortress, 1995), pp. 334–350; David Brakke, *The Gnostics: Myth, Ritual, and Diversity in Early Christianity* (Cambridge, MA: Harvard Univ. Press, 2012).

[7] *Thomas*'s reference to 24 prophets is a bit of a blunder; 24 is the number of Biblical books, not authors.

Explaining Jesus' Crucifixion

Neither Luke
nor Matthew
nor Mark
accuses the
Pharisees or
"the Jews"
in general as
the parties
responsible for
the crucifixion
of Jesus.

HELMUT KOESTER

THE AUTHOR OF THE GOSPEL of Luke was a well-educated gentile Christian. He may have been originally a God-fearer—a gentile who had become an adherent of a Jewish synagogue community before he was converted to the message of Jesus. Luke had an excellent knowledge of the Bible of Israel (the Christian Old Testament) in its Greek translation. He never had any doubt that Jesus, a Jew from Galilee who came from the family of David, belonged to the people of Israel. When the angel announces Jesus' birth to Mary, he says that "God will give to her child the throne of his ancestor David" and that "he will reign over the house of Jacob forever" (Luke 1:32-33). In her song, the "Magnificat," Mary praises God that "he has helped his servant Israel" (Luke 1:54).

It is also only this Gospel that includes the story of Joseph and the pregnant mother of Jesus going to Bethlehem, the city of David.

When Luke wrote his Gospel, some time at the very end of the first century, it was not clear who would emerge as the legitimate heir to the tradition of Israel and its scriptures. There were a number of groups who claimed that they were the only legitimate Israelites: the successors of the Pharisees of the time of Jesus, known as the founders of rabbinic Judaism; the Samaritans, who represented a significant Israelite constituency both in Palestine and in the diaspora; the followers of Jesus, who had just become known under the name Christians; other groups, such as the followers of John the

Baptist; and the remnants of the defeated revolutionaries of the Jewish War of 66-70 against Rome. All these groups appear in Luke's Gospel in relationship to the ministry and fate of Jesus, either as enemies or as sympathizers.

Luke is painfully aware of two facts: (1) Jesus was crucified by the Roman governor Pontius Pilate while the authorities in Jerusalem were only too eager to cooperate with their Roman overlords; (2) followers of Jesus had repeatedly experienced the hostility of Jewish synagogues—a fact recorded by the apostle Paul (see Corinthians 11:24) and by the Gospel of John (9:22). Moreover, in the Book of Acts Luke reports, on the basis of reliable historical information, that Stephen was martyred by the Jews of Jerusalem (Acts 7) and that King Agrippa had the apostle James executed (Acts 12:2). Luke wrote this at a time when Christians were also persecuted by the Roman authorities. This is confirmed by the roughly contemporary letter of the governor of Bithynia, Pliny the Younger (Epistle 10:96), written in about 112 C.E., to the emperor Trajan, in which he reports that he had executed several people because they had confessed that they were Christians and had refused to sacrifice to the emperor. At the same time, the Pharisees were desperately trying to reestablish whatever was left of the scattered Jewish people after the disastrous war with Rome and the destruction of Jerusalem and its Temple.

Jesus, the Jew, had been crucified in Jerusalem. Luke tries to explain in his Gospel why this happened. Rejection by various groups in Israel came early in Jesus' ministry. While Mark's Gospel places Jesus' rejection in Nazareth to a relatively later point in Jesus' ministry (Mark 6:1-6), Luke begins the story of Jesus' career with the account of his rejection there (Luke 4:14-30). Thereafter, in Luke's rewriting of the story, Jesus preaches to the poor and heals the sick freely in Galilee and Judea. But the Pharisees are critical of Jesus' breaking of the Sabbath (Luke 6:2,11). That Jesus is in trouble is apparent again as soon as he sets his mind toward going to Jerusalem: The Samaritans do not allow him to pass through their country (Luke 9:51-55). One would expect that henceforth, in Luke's eyes, the Samaritans would be singled out as especially hostile to Jesus. However, this is not the case. The man who rescues the victim of robbery is identified as a Samaritan (Luke 10:29-37), and of the ten lepers healed by Jesus, the only one who returns to give thanks is a Samaritan (Luke 17:11-19).

It is clear that the Samaritans did not pose a threat to Luke's church, but some of the Jewish people did. One might think that the Pharisees, representing the Jewish leaders in Luke's time, continue to be presented as the enemies of Jesus. They are indeed attacked in the "Speech against the Pharisees" (Luke 11:37-12:1), they complain that Jesus accepts the sinners (Luke 15:2) and a boasting Pharisee is contrasted with the repentant publican in the famous story of Luke 18:9-14.

The Pharisees, however, are not accused of having engineered the death of Jesus. They are never mentioned in the narrative of the trial and execution of Jesus. Rather, it is the leadership of Jerusalem and the high priests who have Jesus arrested by their servants (Luke 22:47-53), and the council of the elders of Jerusalem, high priests and scribes send Jesus to Pilate for execution (Luke 23:1). These are the people who are ultimately responsible for Jesus' death, not the Pharisees.

Thus Luke distances himself from the leaders of Jerusalem at the time of Jesus, but he knows very well that the Pharisees and their successors, the leaders of rabbinic Judaism at his own time, did not have any part in this travesty of justice. To be sure, they are the rivals of the Christians at the time of Luke—and so the Gospel of Luke presents them as Jesus' opponents. But even in the continuation of Luke's story, the Book of the Acts of the Apostles, in which Jewish hostility is mentioned repeatedly, the Pharisees are not described negatively: Gamaliel, their leader in Jerusalem, counsels against further persecution of the apostles (Acts 5:34), some of the Pharisees are mentioned as people who have become believers (Acts 23:9). If Luke describes the leaders of rabbinic Judaism at his own time with the term "Pharisees," it is clear that he does not hold them responsible for Jesus' death or for the persecution of the apostles.

Christians today should take note that neither the Gospels of Luke, Matthew or Mark accuse the Pharisees or "the Jews" in general as the parties responsible for the crucifixion of Jesus, but rather the leaders of Jerusalem, who first collaborated with the Romans and later caused the disastrous revolt of the Jewish people against Rome.

What Really Happened at

The scene has stimulated the imagination of great painters. The light of a full moon accentuates the shadows in a garden at the foot of the Mount of Olives. A lonely figure prays in anguish. Deep in careless sleep, his companions ignore his agony. The swords of the approaching soldiers appear on the horizon. The tension is palpable.

Jesus' prayer in Gethsemane is one of the most soul-wrenching episodes in the Gospels: "My Father, if it is possible, let this cup pass from me. Yet, not as I will but as you (will)" (Matthew 26:39).

Gethsemane?

JEROME MURPHY-O'CONNOR

PHOTO BY THE NORTON GALLERY, PALM SPRINGS, CA. BRIDGEMAN ART LIBRARY, LONDON/SUPERSTOCK.

THE AGONY IN THE GARDEN (previous pages). Disconsolate and abandoned, Jesus weeps as he contemplates his approaching death in this 1889 painting by French artist Paul Gauguin. In the distance appear his disciples, dressed in black; behind them, only the swords are visible of the Roman soldiers ascending the Mount of Olives to arrest him.

Discrepancies abound in the gospel accounts of Jesus' suffering in Gethsemane, leading author Jerome Murphy-O'Connor to ask which version is earliest and why later evangelists altered the story. Repetitions in Mark's account indicated to Murphy-O'Connor that this gospel actually combines two earlier sources. The first and simplest version (labeled Source A) describes a fully human Jesus, in deep agony. As the story was refined over the years, Jesus gradually evolved into a model Christian, calmly accepting his fate in Gethsemane.

If the Transfiguration—the moment when Jesus is mystically transformed in the presence of Moses and Elijah—presents Jesus at his highest, here we see him at his lowest. The radiant Lord who stood erect on a mountain peak now struggles for light in the desolation of night. The disciples who were so attentive at the Transfiguration and begged to prolong the golden moment, do not want to hear or see what is happening to Jesus here.

These contrasting images bear reflection. We like to bask in the glory of the superhuman Jesus

of the Transfiguration.* He is a savior to be proud of. We do not want to deal with a savior consumed by loneliness, desperate fear and uncertainty. These traits are far too human. Nonetheless, this is the real Jesus.

Jesus' struggle in Gethsemane is recounted in all three Synoptic Gospels (Matthew 26:36-46; Mark 14:32-42; and Luke 22:39-46).** There are striking differences, however, which I want to explore here. As we shall see, one gospel actually contains two accounts of Jesus' agony.

What can we say of these varying accounts? Can we determine which was the most original and who copied from whom? Can we reconstruct how the story developed?

Luke's account is much shorter than Mark's or Matthew's (see boxes, pp. 67 and 71). Mark and Matthew depict Jesus praying three times; Luke has only one prayer. The dominant scholarly hypothesis concerning the relationship between Matthew, Mark and Luke claims that when an episode is narrated by all three gospels, Mark, the earliest gospel, is the source; an episode found only in Matthew and Luke, on the other hand, goes back to a hypothetical source scholars call Q.*** Applying this two-source theory to the episode in Gethsemane, we find that Luke, with such a short account, must have severely abbreviated Mark. No other suggestion is seriously considered by scholars.[1]

Such radical surgery on the part of an evangelist would be most unusual, however. He might add or change, but not shorten so drastically.

*See Jerome Murphy-O'Connor, "What Really Happened at the Transfiguration?" *Bible Review*, Fall 1987.

**The term *synoptic,* from the Greek for "seeing together," refers to the fact that Matthew, Mark and Luke share so much material that when printed in three parallel columns, their correspondences can be "seen together" at a glance, as in the box, opposite.

***The common explanation of the name *Q* is that it is short for the German *Quelle,* meaning "source." See Stephen Patterson, "Yes, Virginia, There Is a Q," *Bible Review*, October 1995.

BAYERISCHE STAATSBIBLIOTHEK, MUNICH

"KEEP YE WATCHING!" Jesus urges his disciples as they doze off in Gethsemane. The disciples became increasingly prominent as the story of the agony developed because their presence as eyewitnesses (albeit sleepy ones) became critical to second-generation Christians who wished to verify the source of the gospel stories. Although in Mark's Source A, they are identified only as "his disciples," Mark B names three—James, John and Peter—who are depicted from left to right in this illumination (at left) from a 13th-century English Psalter.

Jesus at Gethsemane: Two Versions

Close scrutiny of Matthew's and Mark's accounts of Jesus at Gethsemane reveals numerous correspondences as well as some tell-tale differences. As laid out here, passages that occur (sometimes word-for-word) in both gospels appear side-by-side. Where there is no close parallel, we've inserted a line space.

According to Mark (14:26,32-42)

(14:26) And having sung a hymn,
they went out to the Mount of Olives.
(32) And they come into the plot of land
the name of which was Gethsemane;
and he says to his disciples, "Sit here

while I pray."
(33) And he takes along Peter,
and James, and John with him,
and he began to be greatly distraught and troubled.
(34) And he says to them,
"My soul is very sorrowful unto death.
Remain here and keep on watching."
(35) And having gone forward a little,
he was falling on the earth
and was praying that

if it is possible
the hour might pass from him.
(36) And he was saying, "Abba, Father,
all things are possible to you.
Take away this cup from me.
But not what I will but what you (will)."
(37) And he comes
and finds them sleeping,
and he says to Peter,
"Simon, are you sleeping?
Were you not strong enough
to watch one hour?
(38) Keep ye watching and praying
lest ye enter into trial.
Indeed the spirit is willing, but the flesh is weak."
(39) And again
having gone away, he prayed, saying
the same word.

(40) And again having come, he found them
sleeping; for their eyes were very burdened,
and they did not know what they should answer him.

(41) And he comes the third time,
and says to them,
"Do you go on sleeping, then, and taking your rest? The
money is paid.
The hour has come.
Behold the Son of Man is given over into the hands of
sinners.
(42) Get up; let us go!
Behold the one who gives me over
has come near."

According to Matthew (26:30,36-46)

(26:30) And having sung a hymn,
they went out to the Mount of Olives.
(36) Then Jesus comes with them into the plot of land
called Gethsemane;
and he says to his disciples, "Sit in this place
until, going away,
I pray there."
(37) And having taken along Peter
and the two sons of Zebedee,
he began to be sorrowful and troubled.
(38) Then he says to them,
"My soul is very sorrowful unto death.
Remain here and keep on watching with me."
(39) And having gone forward a little,
he was falling on his face
praying and saying,
"My Father,
if it is possible,

let this cup pass from me.
Yet, not as I will but as you (will)."
(40) And he comes to the disciples
and finds them sleeping,
and he says to Peter,

"So ye were not strong enough
to watch one hour with me!
(41) Keep ye watching and praying
lest ye enter into trial.
Indeed the spirit is willing, but the flesh is weak."
(42) Again, a second time,
having gone away, he prayed, saying,

"My Father, if it is not possible for this
to pass, let your will be done."
(43) And having come, again he found them
sleeping; for their eyes were burdened.

(44) And having left them, again having gone away, he
prayed a third time, saying the same word again.
(45) Then he comes to the disciples,
and says to them,
"Do you go on sleeping, then, and taking your rest?

Behold the hour has come near,
and the Son of Man is given over into the
hands of sinners.
(46) Get up; let us go!

Behold, there has come near
the one who gives me over."

This suggests that the widely accepted two-source theory is *not* an appropriate framework in which to understand the Gethsemane episode. A very different solution becomes apparent if Mark and Matthew are first analyzed closely.

To help the reader do this, we have printed the text of Mark and Matthew side by side (see box, pp. 67). In the box below we analyze a number of the most significant differences.[2]

The cumulative effect of the variations is to make it appear extremely likely that Matthew copied Mark's account, clarifying it and tidying it up with minor additions and omissions. Hence, if we are to discover what really happened in Gethsemane, we must focus on Mark.

Mark's account introduces us to doublets. Although to theatergoers the word *doublet* may evoke a tight-fitting jacket worn by men in 15th- and 16th-century Europe, to gospel scholars the term is much more mundane; it simply refers to a repeated element.

There are two types of doublets: verbal doublets, a saying or phrase that is repeated in a single gospel; and structural doublets, repeated elements that fulfill the same role in the framework or movement of the narrative.

Mark's account of Jesus in Gethsemane contains a whole series of structural doublets:

- The place to which Jesus and his disciples come appears twice: the Mount of Olives (14:26) and Gethsemane (14:32a).

- Twice Jesus gives an order to his disciples: "Sit here while I pray" (14:32b), and "Remain here and keep watching" (14:34b).

- The subjective state of Jesus is mentioned twice, first in indirect speech, "He began to be greatly distraught and troubled" (14:33a), and then in direct speech, "My soul is very sorrowful unto death" (14:34a).

Which Came First—Matthew or Mark?

Did Matthew copy Mark or the other way round? Clearly the accounts in both gospels are closely related. In many places, they are identical. One must have copied from the other.

To determine which came first, we must look closely at the significant differences. In each case we must ask which author created the difference by adding or subtracting from the source he was using. This involves weighing probabilities. Certainty may elude us. This might seem a very fragile basis on which to reconstruct the life of Jesus, but it is just the sort of judgment we must make all the time in ordering our lives.

Sometimes the judgment is not too difficult. Compare Mark 14:32 with Matthew 26:36, the introduction to the story. Mark says, "they come." Matthew says, "Jesus comes with them." Mark is vague. One has to know that "they" includes Jesus, who is never explicitly mentioned.

In the same verses, Mark has Jesus saying to his disciples, "Sit here," while Matthew has, "Sit in this place." The word "here" in Mark is somewhat confusing because it gives the impression that

Jesus was to stay close to the disciples, whereas in the next verse he moves away. In Matthew, the disciples are told to "sit in this place until, going away, I will pray there."

Both the vagueness of "they come" and the slight confusion caused by "sit here" in Mark's account are rectified in Matthew. Here Jesus is mentioned by name, and Jesus' move away is announced.

Did Matthew solve a problem by changing Mark, or did Mark create a problem by changing Matthew? The choice is an easy one. Matthew was smoothing out Mark.

Now let's compare Mark 14:33 with Matthew 26:37, where Jesus' subjective state is described. Mark says he is "distraught and troubled"; Matthew says "sorrowful and troubled." It is more likely that Matthew changed "distraught" to "sorrowful" to conform with what Jesus says of himself, "My soul is very sorrowful."

The next comparison involves what happens to Jesus. In Mark Jesus collapses, "falling on the earth" (14:35) in an uncontrolled reaction to severe stress. In Matthew Jesus is "falling on his face" (26:39). This

is the classical Jewish posture of prayer, as in Genesis 17:3: "Abram fell on his face" (see also Judges 13:20). Again, our choice is easy. It is most improbable that Mark would defame Jesus by transforming the controlled gesture (prayer) of an entirely self-possessed person into an uncontrolled reaction (despair), whereas it is very likely that Matthew would attempt to improve the image of Jesus by substituting a controlled reaction for an uncontrolled one.

Now let's look at Jesus' prayer. Matthew's version (26:39) is much shorter than Mark's (14:35-36). Our first reaction might be to think that Mark had expanded Matthew.[1] Yet if we look closely at Mark, we immediately notice two internal contradictions. First, Jesus prays that "if it is possible the hour might pass" (Mark 14:35). This "if" contrasts with the certitude in the next verse, in which Jesus says, "All things are possible ... Take away this cup" (Mark 14:36). Second, in these two verses the object of Jesus' prayer shifts from "the hour" to "this cup." These contradictions in Mark are eliminated by Matthew: "If it is possible, let this cup pass from me"

- Similarly, the prayer of Jesus appears twice, again, first in indirect speech, "He was praying that if it is possible, the hour might pass from him" (14:35), and then in direct speech, "Abba, Father, all things are possible to you" (14:35), etc. This prayer is in fact a triplet, but note the vagueness of the third mention, "saying the same words" (14:39).

- The return of Jesus to his sleeping disciples is twice mentioned in virtually the same words: "He comes and finds them sleeping" (14:37), and "Having come, he found them sleeping" (14:40).

- Finally, the theme of handing over is evoked twice: "the Son of Man is given over into the hands of sinners" (14:41), and "the one who gives me over has come near" (14:42).

Such a consistent series of structural doublets permits only one conclusion: Mark's gospel combines two stories.

Can they be reconstructed? A number of scholars have answered yes.[3]

At least one leading New Testament scholar, Raymond Brown, dismisses the whole effort, however: "The theory smacks somewhat of the way modern scholars would work, combining lines from two books propped up on either side of them."[4] In Brown's view, the variety of proposed solutions betrays the futility of the enterprise. In fact, these successive attempts to account for the doublets indicate that scholars of different backgrounds have recognized a real problem that has escaped Brown.

Two aspects of Brown's criticism, however, are not entirely off target. First, scholars have at times permitted idiosyncratic judgments to influence their reconstructions. More importantly, as Brown points out, none of the

---

(Matthew 26:39). This simplification then enables Matthew to create a second prayer, in 26:42, which has no parallel in Mark 14:39.

Matthew's version of events at Gethsemane includes not only two prayers, but also a reference, in 26:44, to a third prayer, in which Jesus says "the same word." The first two prayers of Jesus in Matthew exhibit Jesus' increasing degree of acceptance of his Father's will. In the first (26:39) Jesus still thinks he might be allowed to escape his fate ("If it is possible ..."), but nonetheless submits to his Father's will. In the second prayer (36:42), this hope has been abandoned ("If it is not possible ..."); his submission is complete. If Mark had had this text before him, he would not have changed it.

Mark 14:37 also might have caused some confusion for an early audience. In this passage, Jesus says to Peter, "Simon, are you sleeping?" Only someone familiar with the gospels would know that Simon and Peter were one and the same person ("He gave the name Peter to Simon" [Mark 3:16]). This minor difficulty is compounded

by the pointlessness of his question. We have just been told that Jesus found all the disciples sleeping (Mark 14:37).

As we would expect, Matthew takes care of these difficulties, this time by omitting both the name Simon and the pointless question (Matthew 26:40).[2]

In Mark 14:40, we are told that Jesus found the disciples sleeping. This is immediately followed with the somewhat incongruous statement that "they did not know what they should answer him." If the disciples were asleep, how did they know that Jesus had returned? And why would they reply when Jesus had said nothing?[3] And why would they be troubled over what to answer when they were asleep? Matthew wisely omitted "and they did not know what to answer him" (Matthew 26:43).

Mark 14:41 contains an enigmatic and seemingly meaningless statement without context: "The money is paid" (apechei, in Greek). Scholars fiercely dispute the meaning of this Greek word. Matthew omits it, doubtless because he could not understand it either.[4]

A final bit of confusion or tension appears in Mark 14:41, in which Jesus says that "the hour has come," imply-ing that his arrest is imminent. In the next verse, however, Jesus says that "the one who gives me over [Judas]" has not yet arrived; he has only "come near." Matthew solves this problem by using the same verb, "to come near," both of the hour and of Judas (Matthew 26:45-46).—J.M-O'C.

[1]Matthew does expand Luke in the case of the Lord's Prayer (compare Matthew 6:9-13 and Luke 11:2-4).

[2]In addition, Matthew did not tolerate the tension between the singular "Were you not strong enough to watch one hour?" and the plural "Keep ye watching" (Mark 14:38), so he has Jesus accuse all the disciples (Matthew 26:40).

[3]In Mark there is no departure corresponding to the third return in Mark 14:41. Had there been one in his source, why would Mark have omitted it? Hence, it is Matthew who added the departure (26:44) for the sake of neatness, and moved up the ordinal "third" to match "a second time," which he had inserted in 26:42 to make the numerical series complete.

[4]Raymond E. Brown, The Death of the Messiah: From Gethsemane to the Grave, Anchor Bible Reference Library (New York: Doubleday, 1994), p. 1379.

proposed reconstructions takes into consideration the order of the doublets. The implication is that a reconstruction that *does* follow the order of the doublets would be taken seriously, even by Brown. Such a reconstruction is precisely what I propose (see box, p. 71).

The interlocking stories slide apart without difficulty. Each of the sources combined in Mark is a complete story containing but one prayer of Jesus. When combined, this became two prayers, which Mark increased to three by adding "And again having gone away, he prayed, saying the same word" (14:39), which entailed the insertion of "again" in 14:40 and "He comes the third time" in 14:41. The lack of any content for the third prayer betrays that Mark was interested primarily in the number three, although his reasoning can only be a matter of speculation. One possibility, as Brown

"NOT MY WILL BUT YOURS BE DONE," Jesus prays to God in the Gospel of Luke. In Luke, and in this oil painting by the Italian artist Andrea Mantegna (1431-1506), Jesus serves as an example to Christians by submitting completely to God.

In Mantegna's painting, a troop of cherubim appear in the sky to support Jesus during his fated conflict with the soldiers streaming out of Jerusalem.

suggests, is that the triple failure of the disciples to stay awake was intended to balance the triple denial by Peter (Mark 14:66-72).[5]

Having identified Mark's two sources, the next question is whether we can determine their relative antiquity. Is Source A older than Source B, or the reverse? Several hints suggest that Source A is older.

First, as stories are retold, they often become more specific as ambiguities pointed out by

The Sources of Inspiration

The repetitions in Mark's account of the Agony suggest to author Jerome Murphy-O'Connor that Mark was working from two earlier sources, referred to here as A and B. Mark apparently felt that he should not omit anything found in his sources, and thus combined them. Luke, too, had access to Sources A and B and tried to be faithful to them, but he strove to avoid repetition. That is one reason why his account is so much shorter than Mark's.

Sources A and B are reconstituted in full at left. The phrases and ideas Luke borrowed from these sources appear in italics. As Luke wove together passages from Sources A and B, he sometimes altered the phrasing and the order. So that you can see precisely what changes Luke made, in the central column we've isolated the passages that Luke adapted from Sources A and B and aligned them, side-by-side, with the originals (in italics in the left column).

In the right column, we see Luke's full gospel account of the Agony, with the material he borrowed from A and B in italics.

The Sources of Mark and Luke (derived from Mark 14:26,32-42)

SOURCE A

(14:26b) They went out *to the Mount of Olives*. (32b) And he says to *his disciples*, "Sit here while I pray."
(33b) And *he began to be greatly distraught and troubled*.
(35) And *having gone forward a little*, he was falling on the earth, and was praying that *if it is possible*, the hour might pass from him. (40) Having come [],* *he found them sleeping, for their eyes were very burdened*.
(41) [] And he says to them, "*Do you go on sleeping*, then, and taking your rest? The money is paid. The hour has come. []
(42) *Get up*; let us go. Behold the one who gives me over has come near."

SOURCE B

(14:32a) They come to the plot of land the name of which was Gethsemane. (33a) And he takes along Peter, and James, and John with him. (34) And he says to them, "My soul is very sorrowful unto death. Remain here and keep watching." (36) And he was saying, "Abba, *Father,* all things are possible to you. *Take away this cup from me. But not what I will but what you (will)*."
(37) And he comes and finds them sleeping, and he says to **Peter**, "Simon, are you sleeping? Where you not strong enough to watch one hour? (38) *Keep ye watching and praying lest ye enter into trial.* Indeed the spirit is willing but the flesh is weak."
(40b) And they did not know what they should answer him.

*Brackets [] indicate where Mark's gospel contains material not found in Sources A and B.

What Luke Took from the Sources

LUKE'S USE OF SOURCE A

(22:39a) *to the Mount of Olives*
(39b) *the disciples*

(44) *Being in agony ... his sweat became as if drops of blood falling down to the earth*
(41) *he drew away from them as if a stone's throw*
(42b) *if you desire*
(45) *he found them asleep for sorrow*
(46) *Why do you sleep?*

(46b) *having stood up*

LUKE'S USE OF SOURCE B

(22:42a) *Father*
(42c) *Take away this cup from me*
(42d) *Nevertheless, not my will but yours be done*

(40) *Keep on praying not to enter into trial*
(46) *Keep on praying lest ye enter into trial*

Luke's Finished Account

Luke 22:39-46
(22:39) And having gone out, he proceeded according to his custom *to the Mount of Olives*; and *the disciples* too followed him. (40) And being at the place, he said to them, "*Keep on praying not to enter into trial.*" (41) And *he drew away from them as if a stone's throw*; and having knelt he was praying, (42) saying, "*Father, if you desire, take away this cup from me. Nevertheless, not my will but yours be done.*" (43) But an angel from heaven appeared to him, strengthening him. (44) And *being in agony*, he was praying more earnestly. And *his sweat became as if drops of blood falling down to the earth*. (45) And having stood up from prayer, having come to the disciples, *he found them asleep for sorrow;* (46) and he said to them, "*Why do you sleep? Having stood up, keep on praying lest you enter into trial.*"

the audience are clarified. This appears to have happened in Mark.

Source A, for example, mentions "the Mount of Olives" (14:26b) and "his disciples" (14:32b). These give rise to obvious questions: Precisely where on the Mount of Olives, which is quite a large area? And which disciples? Both of these questions are answered by Source B, which locates the episode in "a plot of land called Gethsemane" (14:32a) and names the key disciples as "Peter and James and John" (14:33a). Source B, therefore, is more developed than Source A.

Second, as a general rule, stories that focus on Jesus while leaving the disciples in the background are older than stories that emphasize the disciples' presence. The earliest stories were told by eyewitnesses who knew what they had seen. The second generation of Christians, on the other hand, had to rely on what they were told; they needed to be reassured that those who told the story knew what they were talking about. Consequently, later stories tend to stress that first-generation disciples *were* present and involved and therefore were able to report accurately.

Thus, in Source A, Jesus separates himself from his disciples. He tells them, "Sit here while I pray" (14:32b), and moves away (14:35a). In Source B, however, Jesus exhorts his disciples to "keep watching" (14:34b).[6] Jesus' movement away is not mentioned explicitly in Source B. Rather, his departure has to be inferred from his return to the disciples in 14:37. The need for Jesus to be observed is apparent in Source B, although it was frustrated by the sleep of the disciples. The editor's respect for his source did not permit him to pretend that the disciples remained wide awake, but he used their slumber for a little moral lesson, "Watch and pray lest ye enter into trial" (14:38), which deflects attention from Jesus to the needs of the early Church. On this basis, too, Source A appears to be earlier.

Let us look more closely now at the contents of Source A. It is perfectly plausible that Jesus and his disciples should head for the Mount of Olives after an evening meal in Jerusalem. They were poor Galileans who could not afford to lodge in a city crowded with wealthier pilgrims. The resident population of Jerusalem at that time has been estimated at between 40,000[7] and 60,000.[8] During pilgrimage feasts, the population swelled to about 180,000.[9] Space in the city, therefore, was at a premium.

The close relationship between Jesus and the family of Martha, Mary and Lazarus, who lived in the village of Bethany (John 11:1-3), suggests that Jesus made his base with them when he came to Jerusalem.[10] It was only 2 miles from the city (John 11:18). Jesus had to climb the Mount of Olives each day to reach the city and again on his return at night (Mark 11:11-12). On the night of the Agony, Jesus and his disciples were returning to Bethany on the eastern slope of the Mount of Olives: "And every day he was teaching in the Temple, but at night he went out and lodged on the Mount of Olives" (Luke 21:37).

The traditional site of Gethsemane has much to recommend its authenticity. When the church historian and bishop Eusebius of Caesarea wrote his *Onomasticon* (an alphabetic list of biblical places with descriptions of their history and geography) at some point between 324 and 336, Gethsemane was already a well-established place of prayer, on the basis of a tradition transmitted by the Christian community of Jerusalem, which had never abandoned the city.[11] The site now marked by the Church of All Nations is in fact located at the easiest point to start climbing up the Mount of Olives. Today three roads radiate upwards from that point and come together on the ridge that leads to Bethany. The path that Jesus and his disciples intended to follow is undoubtedly that marked by an ancient flight of rock-cut steps, which may still be seen in the garden of the Russian church of Saint Mary Magdelene,[12] just upslope from the Church of All Nations.

On reaching the Mount of Olives, Source A tells us, Jesus "began to be deeply distraught and troubled" (14:33b). Exegetes have struggled to find adequate words to bring out the force of the two Greek verbs used here, *ekthambeô* and *adêmoneô*.

Exthambeô is often translated "amazed," but the connotations of "amazement" in current English (entertained, amused) make it inappropriate. The context here demands the element of shock that the verb carries in Mark 10:24 and 16:5-6. It is a matter of "terrified surprise,"[13] a dawning awareness that produces "shuddering horror."[14]

The usual translation of *adêmoneô* is "to be distressed, troubled," but the connotations of the verb established by usage go much further. One commentator has noted that the term "describes the confused, restless, half-distracted state, which is produced by physical derangement or by mental

SUPERSTOCK

distress...[T]he primary idea of the word will be loathing and discontent."[15]

In short, Jesus began to be filled with appalling dread.

The only explanation of this paroxysm of instinctive revulsion is that Jesus had become

"AN ANGEL FROM HEAVEN"—referred to first in Luke's account of the Agony (Luke 22:44)—comforts Jesus in this painting by the Danish artist Carl Heinrich Bloch (1834-1890). Luke mentions the angel's presence even before describing Jesus' suffering, thereby ensuring that his readers would not take Jesus' agony to heart: All is unfolding according to God's plan.

"TAKE AWAY THIS CUP," Jesus prays in Luke 22:39-46, figuratively asking God to end his suffering. Rather than falling to the ground in anguish as in Mark's Source A, in Luke and in this 15th-century bronze relief by Donatello, Jesus appears as a model Christian, praying on his knees—the standard position for prayer among Christians by Luke's time.

Sculpted for the pulpit of the Church of San Lorenzo in Florence, the relief portrays the angel who strengthens Jesus (Luke 22:44) as proffering Jesus a cup—a chalice—so that Jesus appears as a churchgoer, kneeling to receive the Eucharist at mass. In the foreground, 11 disciples, heavy with sleep, miss the miraculous event transpiring behind them.

aware that his death was imminent. But why was the impact so great at this point? I am convinced that he had already come to terms with his death, realizing that his death would be *the* saving event in God's plan for humanity.* After all, Jesus had previously foreseen and

* See Murphy-O'Connor, "What Really Happened at the Transfiguration?" *Bible Review*, Fall 1987, p. 18.

predicted his death (Mark 8:31, 9:31, 10:33-34). Something must have happened in Mark 14:33 to bring his awareness of his death to a different level. What provoked the shocking shift from the theoretical to the real—a shift that almost broke Jesus?

The most probable answer lies in the setting. Jesus reached the foot of the Mount of Olives by the Kidron Valley (John 18:1). Today both sides of the valley are lined with tombs, Muslim on the west and Jewish on the east, because both religions believe the valley to be the place of the Last Judgment. By Jesus' time, what is now the village of Silwan was a great graveyard.[16] Between it and Gethsemane, two huge tomb monuments (the so-called tombs of Absalom and Zechariah) marked catacombs cut into the cliff.[17] They would have been perfectly visible in the full moon of Passover. Jesus had been under direct threat since Caiaphas had decreed that "one man should die for the people" (John 11:50). Weighed down with apprehension, the sight of the tombs lining his route forced the thought of death from his head to his heart. He became profoundly disturbed at the thought, "It might be tonight!"

Jesus manages to control himself sufficiently to tell his disciples to wait while he struggles for self-mastery in prayer. Then, overwhelmed by the hidden fears surging over him, he collapses on the ground.[18] Does he pray? "If it is possible." Jesus' words in Mark 14:35b suggest he is not even sure that God can help him. His is almost a cry of despair over the nearness of the "hour" of his destiny. The prayer is followed by silence. God has not answered.

Somehow Jesus finds the internal strength to pull himself together. He accepts his destiny while his weary disciples sleep. His questions mock their self-absorption.

If the disciples were asleep, how did they know what was happening to Jesus?[19] In other words, where did the information in Source A come from? It is difficult to imagine that it came from Jesus himself. He was arrested immediately afterwards, and there is no hint that he had any opportunity to speak to his disciples before he was put to death. Even if he had, they probably would have talked of other matters.

If Jesus was not the source, then the only possibility is that certain disciples projected onto Jesus the emotions that they imagined they would experience if they suddenly realized their death was imminent.[20] As the followers of a crucified criminal, they knew that they were walking a dangerous path and must have reflected frequently on how *they* would react if threatened with death. The disciples who composed Source A were honest with themselves. They did not flatter themselves about their courage in a crisis. They understood that mastery of the deep-rooted instinct of self-preservation would not come easily and presumed that Jesus felt the same way. They fully accepted his humanity. He was like them in all things except sin (Hebrews 2:17, 4:15). They did not imagine Jesus as a superman, with no fears or frailties.

The intensely human Jesus revealed by Source A—a leader on the verge of a nervous breakdown—proved to be more than some other Christians could accept. In consequence, they wrote a different version of what happened in Gethsemane, which has survived as Source B.

Source B lacks the explicit statement that Jesus "became filled with terrified surprise and distressed from shock" (Mark 14:33b).[21] Instead, in Source B Jesus speaks for himself: "My soul is very sorrowful unto death" (Mark 14:34a). On the surface this appears to convey the same emotional state.[22] In fact, ancient readers (or listeners) would have recognized the allusions to Psalm 41:6,12, "Why are you very sorrowful, my soul, and why do you distress me?" and, perhaps, to Jonah 4:9, "I am so weighed down by sorrow, I want to die." In Source B Jesus is sufficiently composed to make scriptural allusions.

This is a radical shift away from the mood of Source A. The man in intense agony has become calm enough to quote Scripture. The individual suffering a private hell has been replaced by a familiar religious type, either the just man of the Psalms, who suffers persecution yet is sustained by God,[23] or the weary prophet, who begs for release by death.[24]

Jesus' prayer in Source B (Mark 14:36) contains no hint of the anguished doubt so vivid in Source A (Mark 14:35). In Source B, Jesus, addressing God with the utmost formality as "Abba, Father," replaces doubt with certitude: "All things are possible to you."[25]

The final element in Jesus' prayer in Source B is, "But not what I will but what you (will)" (Mark 14:36). Nothing remotely resembling this petition appears in Source A. It is the perfect submission to the will of God that is expected of all Christians. Such concentration on the way believers should live has taken us a long way from the stark struggle of Source A. The Jesus of Source B is calm and collected, introducing scriptural allusions to stimulate the theological reflection of his disciples and offering them an example and advice for the living of their Christian lives.

Mark must have been aware of how different the two Gethsemane stories were. Why then did he combine his two sources rather than choose between them? The simplest answer is that he was not willing to throw away a scrap of the tradition about Jesus. He could see no justification for preserving Source B at the expense of Source A, or vice versa. Human nature being what it is, one might suspect that Mark personally preferred Source B, but he also knew his audience and recognized that, when combined, Source A would be interpreted in the light of Source B.

Having examined both of Mark's sources,

we are now in a position to appreciate Luke's shorter narrative, which resembles Sources A and B individually to the extent that each has only one prayer of Jesus (see box, p. 71), as opposed to the three prayers in the final versions of both Mark and Matthew.

Luke's text is an extraordinary combination of elements that refle ct different parts of Source A and Source B of Mark (see box, p. 71). It would appear that Luke tried to be faithful to both sources, but without combining them as Mark did.

Luke's version also contains two distinctive elements: Jesus' bloodlike sweat (Luke 22:44), and the angel (Luke 22:43). Some scholars argue that these elements were added a century or so after Luke's gospel was composed. This is not the place to debate this highly technical problem, but I am inclined to agree with Brown that on balance the evidence favors the view that they always belonged to the gospel.[26]

A sweat of blood is not physically impossible.[27] Luke, however, does not speak of a sweat of blood but of a sweat so profuse that it was *like* blood The cause of this sweat was Jesus' "agony." To us this suggests intense suffering, but to a first-century reader it would have evoked a struggle for victory.[28] Luke mentions the drenching perspiration to underline the intense internal struggle that demanded every ounce of Jesus' concentration and energy.

Where Mark's Source A presents a Jesus who is "deeply distraught and troubled," Luke, with his refined sense of graphic artistry, is much less explicit, simply referring to bloodlike sweat. And Luke betrays his preference for Source B by introducing the angel before mentioning the bloodlike sweat. Someone interested only in telling the story would have used the natural order of problem (the "agony") followed by solution (the appearance of the angel). By mentioning the angel first, Luke ensured that his readers would not take Jesus' "agony" too seriously. After all, what could possibly happen to Jesus when a powerful heavenly figure was there to comfort and fortify him?

Further evidence for Luke's preference for the perspective of Source B is provided by Jesus' posture as he prays. As we have noted, in Mark 14:35 Jesus collapses; in Matthew 26:39 Jesus assumes the classic Jewish position of reverence, with his face to the ground. Luke, for his part, has Jesus "drop to his knees," a totally controlled posture that had become the standard position

for Christian prayer when Luke wrote.[29]

The angel in Luke's version softens God's silence in Source A and God's refusal to answer Jesus' prayer in Source B. The divine response in Luke is still negative, but God relents to the extent of strengthening Jesus to drink the cup of suffering: "An angel from heaven appeared to him, strengthening him" (Luke 22:43).

Reading the accounts in the probable order of composition, we see Jesus' acceptance of his fate becoming progressively more perfect. The culmination of this process is to be found in John's version.

John usually does not repeat events that have been adequately described by the other evangelists, but evokes them in a different context by means of a highly specific allusion.[30] That is the case here. John anticipates Jesus' prayer in Gethsemane: "Now is my soul distressed, and what shall I say, 'Father, save me from this hour? No, for this purpose I have come to this hour. Father, glorify your name!' Then a voice came from heaven, 'I have glorified it, and I will glorify it again!' The crowd standing by heard it and said that it had thundered. Others said, 'An angel had spoken to him'" (John 12:27-29).

The connection of this passage with the Gethsemane episode in the other gospels is clear:[31] "My soul is distressed" evokes Psalm 41:6,12 in exactly the same way as Mark's "My soul is very sorrowful" (Mark 14:34a); a petition concerning "the hour" resembles Mark's "if it is possible 'the hour' might pass from him" (Mark 14:35); and the angel appears in Luke's account (Luke 22:43).

In John's gospel, Jesus' submission to the will of his Father is so perfect that he will not even ask for deliverance. He refuses to utter the prayer attributed to him by Matthew, Mark and Luke. Jesus explicitly acknowledges that throughout his ministry the divine will has guided him to this moment. Why should he at the last minute refuse the whole purpose of his life? On the contrary, he glorifies the Father, and this time there is a positive response from heaven: "I have glorified it, and will glorify it again" (John 12:28). With this reference to a past moment of glorification, John evokes the Transfiguration, which he does not describe explicitly elsewhere.[3]

With John we have come very far from the lonely figure in the moonlight-dappled garden, whose body and spirit momentarily rebelled against what he knew to be the inexorable plan of his Father for the salvation of humanity. ⬛

[1] Thus, for example, Joseph A. Fitzmyer, *The Gospel According to Luke,* Anchor Bible 28A (Garden City, NY: Doubleday, 1985), p. 1438.

[2] To bring out even the most minute differences between the gospels, a very literal translation has been used. It is taken from Raymond E. Brown, *The Death of the Messiah: From Gethsemane to the Grave,* Anchor Bible Reference Library (New York: Doubleday, 1994), pp. 1583-1602.

[3] Their proposals are listed below. Elements added by Mark when he combined the two sources are not taken into account. For Source A, Rudolf Thiel (*Drei Markus-Evangelien* [Berlin: De Gruyter, 1938], p. 23) includes 14:33,34,35a,36,37,38; Emanuel Hirsch (*Die Frühgeschichte des Evangeliums, I. Das Werden des Markus-Evangeliums* [Tübingen: Vandenhoeck & Ruprecht, 1951], pp. 156-157), 14:34,35,37,42; Karl Georg Kuhn ("Jesus in Gethsemane," *Evangelische Theologie* 12 [1951-1952], pp. 266-267), 14:32,35,40,41; Pierre Benoit ("Les outrages à Jésus Prophète," in *Neotestamentica et Patristica, Festschrift for O. Cullmann* [Leiden: Brill, 1962], p. 103 n. 8), 14:32a,34b, 32b,35,[40-41a],41b,42; Marie-Emile Boismard (*Synopse des Quatres Evangiles en Français,* II [Paris: Cerf, 1972], pp. 392-393), 14:26,32b, 35a,36,40, 41; J. Warren Holleran (*The Synoptic Gethsemane,* Analecta Gregoriana 191 [Rome: Gregorian University, 1973], p. 144), 14:32,33b,35,40,41,42a; Xavier Léon-Dufour ("Jésus à Géthsemani. Essai de lecture synchronique," *Science et esprit* 31 [1979], p. 251), 14:32,33b,35,40,50; David Stanley (*Jesus in Gethsemane: The Early Church Reflects on the Suffering of Jesus* [New York: Paulist, 1980], pp. 108-111), 14:32,33b,35,40,41,42a For Source B, Thiel includes 14:32,39,35b,40,41a; Hirsch, 14:32,36,38a,41; Kuhn, 14:33,34,36,37,38; Benoit, 14:33,34ac,39,36,37,38; Boismard, 14:32a, 33,34b,38,39,36,37; Holleran, 14:33a,34,39a, 36,37,38; Léon-Dufour, 14:33a,34,36,37; Stanley, 14:26b,33a, 34,36,37,38.

[4] Brown, *Death of the Messiah,* p. 221.

[5] Brown, *Death of the Messiah,* p. 204.

[6] This tendency is accentuated by Matthew's addition, "keep watching *with me*" (v. 38).

[7] Magen Broshi, "La population de l'ancienne Jérusalem," *Revue biblique* 82 (1975), p. 13. He bases his estimate on the average number of inhabitants per acre, in contrast to Wilkinson (see next note), who bases his estimate on the city's water supply.

[8] John Wilkinson, "Ancient Jerusalem—Its Water Supply and Population," *Palestine Exploration Quarterly* 106 (1974), p. 49.

[9] See Joachim Jeremias, *Jerusalem in the Time of Jesus—An Investigation into Economic and Social Conditions During the New Testament Period* (London: SCM, 1969), p. 84. Jeremias bases his estimate on an average of 18,000 sacrificial lambs multiplied by an average of 10 at each meal (p. 83).

[10] See Sylvester Saller, *Excavations at Bethany (1949-53)* (Jerusalem: Franciscan Press, 1957).

[11] See Jerome Murphy-O'Connor "Pre-Constantinian Christian Jerusalem," in Anthony O'Mahony, Göran Gunner, Kevork Hintlian, eds., *The Christian Heritage in the Holy Land* (London: Scorpian Cavandish, 1995), pp. 15-17.

[12] Louis-Hugues Vincent and Felix-Marie Abel, *Jerusalem nouvelle* (Paris: Gabalda, 1914), p. 305.

[13] Henry Barclay Swete, *The Gospel According to St. Mark* (London: Macmillan, 1908), p. 342.

[14] Brown, *Death of the Messiah,* p. 153.

[15] Joseph Barber Lightfoot, *Saint Paul's Epistle to the Philippians* (London: Macmillan, 1908), p. 123.

[16] David Ussishkin, *The Village of Silwan* (Jerusalem: Israel Exploration Society and Yad Izhak Ben-Zvi, 1993).

[17] For description and dating, see Kay Prag, *Jerusalem,* Blue Guide (London: Black, 1989), pp. 247-51.

[18] So, rightly, David Stanley, *Jesus in Gethsemane,* p. 134. Brown reluctantly concedes that Jesus' action complements what is said of his distraught state, but then says that Matthew "slightly softens Mark's picture of Jesus' distress" (*Death of the Messiah,* p. 165). In fact, Matthew changes the picture completely (as does Luke) by substituting a controlled action for an uncontrolled one.

[19] The question is raised by Stanley (*Jesus in Gethsemane,* p. 140), but not really answered.

[20] Brown says that "there was an early Christian memory or understanding that Jesus struggled with and prayed to God about his impending death" (*Death of the Messiah,* p. 177, cf. p. 225), but does not say where either came from. When he wrote his commentary on John 12:27-28, Brown suggested, "Since there were no witnesses to report the prayer of Jesus during the agony (the disciples were asleep at a distance), the tendency would be to fill in the skeletal framework of the Gethsemane scene with prayers and sayings uttered by Jesus at other times" (*The Gospel According to John (I-XIII),* Anchor Bible 29 (Garden City, NY: Doubleday, 1966), p. 471.

[21] Stanley's translation (*Jesus in Gethsemane,* p. 108).

[22] It is paraphrased "My sorrow is so great that it almost overwhelms me" in Christopher S. Mann, *Mark,* Anchor Bible 27 (New York: Doubleday, 1986), p. 587.

[23] J. Warren Halloran, *The Synoptic Gethsemane,* Analecta Gregoriana 191 (Rome: Gregorian University, 1973), p. 207.

[24] David Daube, "Death as a Release in the Bible," *Novum Testamentum* 5 (1962), pp. 96-98. This study also evokes Moses (Numbers 11:15), Elijah (1 Kings 19:4) and Jeremiah (Jeremiah 20:14-18).

[25] Cf. Mark 10:27.

[26] Brown, *Death of the Messiah,* pp. 180-186.

[27] Brown cites medical evidence of "instances of hemaidrosis, involving intense dilation of subcutaneous capillaries that burst into the sweat glands. The blood then clots and is carried to the surface of the skin by the sweat" (*Death of the Messiah,* pp. 185).

[28] "But it is also well attested for a state of mind associated with fear or anguish because of some impending, uncertain experience or phenomenon" (Fitzmyer, *The Gospel According to Luke,* p. 1444).

[29] Precisely these words are used of the prayers of Peter (Acts 9:40), Paul (Acts 20:36) and the community at Tyre (Acts 21:5). Kneeling while praying was not unknown among the Jews; see 1 Kings 8:54 (which, however, contradicts 1 Kings 8:22!) and Daniel 6:10.

[30] For example, John's version of the Last Supper (John 13:1-20) does not contain the institution of the Eucharist (Mark 14:22-25 = Matthew 26:26-29 = Luke 22:15-20), but in the discourse on the bread of life (John 6:26-59), which takes place much earlier in the ministry of Jesus, John evokes the Eucharist by the words "the bread which I shall give for the life of the world is my flesh ... [U]nless you eat the flesh of the Son of Man and drink his blood, you have no life in you; he who eats my flesh and drinks my blood has eternal life" (John 6:51-54).

[31] Brown, *The Gospel According to John,* p. 470.

[32] Brown, *The Gospel According to John,* p. 476.

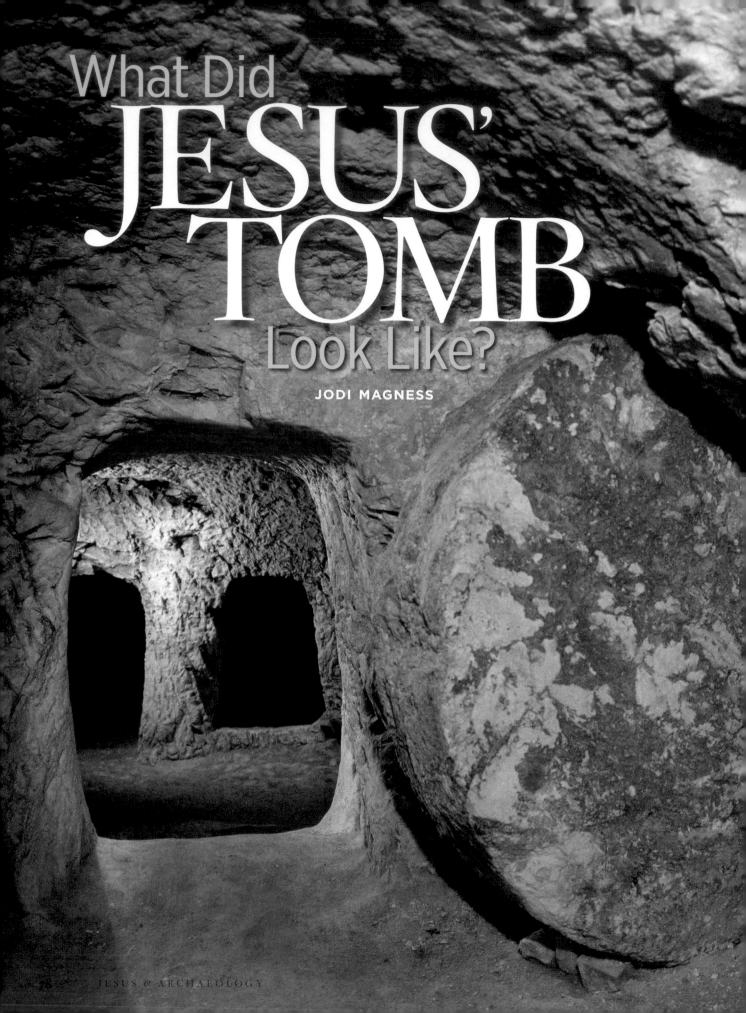

What Did
JESUS' TOMB
Look Like?

JODI MAGNESS

ACCORDING TO THE GOSPELS, JESUS died and was removed from the cross on a Friday afternoon, the eve of the Jewish Sabbath. A wealthy follower named Joseph of Arimathea requested Pontius Pilate's permission to remove Jesus' body from the cross and bury him before sundown, in accordance with Jewish law. Because there was no time to prepare a grave before the Sabbath, Joseph placed Jesus' body in his own family's tomb.

The reliability of the Gospel accounts—which were written a generation or two after Jesus' death—is debated by scholars. Most discussions have focused on literary and historical considerations, such as the composition dates of the Gospels and internal contradictions and differences between them. Here, I will consider the account of Jesus' burial in light of the archaeological evidence. I believe that the Gospel accounts accurately reflect the manner in which the Jews of ancient Jerusalem buried their dead in the first century.

Wealthy Jews in ancient Jerusalem buried their dead in tombs cut into the bedrock slopes around the city. These rock-cut tombs were used by Jerusalem's Jewish elite only in times when they enjoyed an autonomous or semi-autonomous status. With few exceptions, the tombs were located outside the walls of the city. Each tomb was used by a family over the course of several generations, as reflected in the Biblical expression "He slept and was gathered to his fathers" (Judges 2:10; 2 Chronicles 34:28, etc.)

When a member of the family died, the body was wrapped in a shroud, sometimes placed in a coffin and laid in the tomb, even if the bones were later collected and placed elsewhere (either in a separate repository, as in the First Temple period, or, in a later period, in a bone box called an ossuary). Because of the expense associated with hewing a burial cave out of bedrock, however, only upper class and upper-middle class Jerusalemites could afford rock-cut tombs. The poorer members of Jerusalem's population apparently disposed of their dead in a manner that has left few traces in the archaeological record, for example in simple individual trench graves dug into the ground.

Rock-cut tombs of the late First Temple period (eighth-seventh century B.C.E.) typically consist of one or more burial chambers entered through a small, unadorned opening cut into the bedrock. Each burial chamber is lined with rock-cut benches along three sides on which the bodies of the deceased were laid. Frequently a pit carved beneath one of the benches was used as a repository for the bones of earlier burials; when the benches became filled with bodies, the remains (skeletons and grave gifts) were placed in the repository to make space for new burials on the burial benches.

An undisturbed repository in the Ketef Hinnom cemetery (overlooking the Hinnom Valley, northwest of the Old City) contained large numbers of skeletons as well as the burial gifts that accompanied them, including ceramic vases and oil lamps, jewelry, seals, a rare early coin and two silver amulets.* Many of the decorative elements in these burial caves, such as the carved headrests on the benches, reflect Egyptian styles transmitted directly from Egypt or through Phoenician intermediaries. We shall see foreign cultural influences and fashions again reflected in burials of a later period.

After the destruction of Jerusalem and Solomon's Temple in 586 B.C.E., archaeological evidence for Jewish burial caves reappears only in the Hasmonean period, when Jerusalem again came under Jewish rule. As a result of the Maccabean Revolt in

"ON THE FIRST DAY of the week, very early in the morning, the women took the spices they had prepared and went to the tomb. They found the stone rolled away from the tomb…" (Luke 24:1-2). The Synoptic Gospels (Matthew, Mark and Luke) agree that Jesus was laid in a tomb that had a rolling stone closing the entrance, much like this Herodian-era tomb from the necropolis under the Convent of the Sisters of Nazareth in Nazareth. The Gospels also record that when the women came to anoint the body, the stone had been rolled away. In the accompanying article, author Jodi Magness discusses the burial customs of first-century C.E. Jerusalem and finds that the Biblical account of Jesus' burial matches what we know from archaeological evidence.

*See Gabriel Barkay, "News from the Field: The Divine Name Found in Jerusalem," *Biblical Archaeology Review*, March/April 1983.

the mid-second century B.C.E., an independent Jewish kingdom ruled by the Hasmonean dynasty was established by the brothers of Judah Maccabee. Although Judah Maccabee and his brothers were renowned for their opposition to the introduction of Hellenistic (Greek) culture, the Hasmonean rulers nevertheless Hellenized their kingdom soon after its establishment. This is perhaps best illustrated by the monumental family tomb and victory memorial built by Simon (Judah Maccabee's youngest brother) in their hometown of Modiin, in which he interred the remains of his parents and brothers. Although no archaeological remains of this tomb survive, the descriptions of ancient literary sources, including the Book of Maccabees and the first-century C.E. Jewish historian Josephus, leave little doubt that it was inspired by the tomb of King Mausolus of Caria—the so-called Mausoleum of Halicarnassus (now modern Bodrum on the southwest coast of

HEADRESTS ADORN a burial bench in a late Iron Age (eighth-sixth century B.C.E.) tomb at Ketef Hinnom, northwest of Jerusalem's Old City. Tombs in ancient Jerusalem were a family affair mainly for the city's well-to-do. Iron Age tombs were hewn in the bedrock around the city and consisted of several chambers containing rock-cut benches upon which the bodies of the deceased were placed. After the bodies had decomposed, the bones would be removed from the benches and placed in a pit or repository to make way for new burials. In the photo on page 81, student excavators with their heads in the stone headrests demonstrate how the bodies were laid out in the First Temple period. The inset phot, left, from the tombs at the École Biblique in Jerusalem, shows a headrest carved like the head of the Egyptian goddess Hathor.

RICHARD NOWITZ

WWW.HOLYLANDPHOTOS.ORG

Turkey)—which was one of the seven wonders of the ancient world:

> And Simon built a monument over the grave of his father and his brothers, and made it high so that it could be seen, with polished stone on back and front. And he erected seven pyramids in a row, for his father and his mother and his four brothers. And he made devices for these, setting up great trophies of armor for an everlasting memorial, and beside the armor carved prows of ships, so that they could be seen by all who sailed the sea. Such was the monument that he built at Modiin, and that still stands today" (1 Maccabees 13:27-30).

> However, Simon sent some to the city Basca to bring away his brother's bones, and buried them in their own city Modiin; and all the people made great lamentation over him. Simon also erected a very large monument for his father and his brethren, of white and polished stone, and raised it to a great height, and so as to be seen a long way off, and made cloisters about it, and set up pillars, which were of one stone apiece; a work it was wonderful to see. Moreover, he built seven pyramids also for his parents and his brethren, one for each of them, which were made very surprising, both for their largeness and beauty, and which have been preserved to this day (Josephus, *Antiquities* 13.6.6).

These descriptions indicate that, like the Mausoleum at Halicarnassus, the tomb of the Maccabees consisted of a tall podium with a temple-like building surrounded by columns and capped by a pyramidal roof (or in the case of the tomb of the Maccabees, seven pyramids, one for each family member, including Simon himself). As archaeologist Andrea Berlin has pointed out, none of these features is found in earlier Jewish or Phoenician tombs in Palestine.[1] The tomb of the Maccabees retains the ancient tradition of family burial in a rock-cut tomb but adds Greek-style exterior decoration and a monumental marker. The Jews referred to such monumental tomb markers as a *nefesh* (Hebrew for "soul").

Hellenistic influence on the Hasmoneans can also be seen in their adoption of Greek names, beginning with Simon's immediate successor, who preferred the Greek name John Hyrcanus over his Hebrew name Yohanan.[2]

A Hasmonean-period tomb in Jerusalem called Jason's Tomb demonstrates that Jerusalem's elite soon imitated the new tomb style introduced by Simon. Jason's Tomb is located in the western Jerusalem neighborhood of Rehavia[3] and is so called because a graffito incised on one of the walls asks the visitor to lament the death of Jason.[4] Jason's Tomb continues the earlier tradition of rock-cut burial caves in Jerusalem, but with several Hellenistic innovations: A large stone pyramid (an example of a *nefesh*) was constructed above the tomb. The tomb was approached through a series of long, open courtyards

leading to a porch in the front of the tomb that was supported by a single Doric (Greek-style) column. This column was set between the projecting ends of the porch walls (an arrangement described in Greek architecture as *in-antis*; the *antae* are the ends of the porch walls). The porch gives access to two rooms: a burial chamber and a charnel room. Instead of having rock-cut benches like the First Temple period tombs, the burial chamber in Jason's Tomb has *loculi* (in Hebrew *kokhim*). *Loculi* are long niches that were cut into the walls, each for an individual burial. Like the pyramidal marker and the porch with a column, *loculi* reflect Hellenistic influence. *Loculi* are common in tombs at Alexandria in Egypt, which was the cultural center of the Hellenistic world. They make their first known appearance in Palestine at Maresha, a site south of Jerusalem that was inhabited by Hellenized Phoenicians from Sidon and by Idumeans (descendants of the Biblical Edomites).

Instead of depositing the remains of earlier burials in a pit or repository (to make room for more burials), as in the First Temple period tombs, the bones cleared out of the *loculi* in Jason's Tomb were placed in a charnel room. Beginning in about 20-10 B.C.E., the practice of placing bones from the *loculi* in a charnel room or pit changed to placing the bones in stone boxes

ONE OF THE SEVEN WONDERS of the ancient world, the Mausoleum of Halicarnassus (above, left) was the inspiration for the grand Hellenistic tomb erected by Simon Maccabee, younger brother of Judah Maccabee, for the family tomb and victory memorial he erected in Modiin, the family's home town. The Modiin tomb, in turn, helped spread Hellenistic styles to Jerusalem tombs in the Hasmonean Period, the era of Maccabee-family rule (152-37 B.C.E.). Neither the Mausoleum nor the tomb of the Maccabees survive, but other examples, such as Jason's Tomb (opposite) in central modern Jerusalem and the tomb of Zacharias (above, right) from the necropolis in the Kidron Valley preserve Hellenistic architectural elements. Jason's Tomb, so called because it contains a graffito with that name, was built with a Doric column *in antis*—between two walls of the porch. A pyramidal roof and *loculi* (niches carved in the walls to hold the bodies) are also Greek touches. The Tomb of Zacharias, too, has a pyramidal roof, but is decorated with a façade of engaged Ionic columns.

called ossuaries. Ossuaries remained common in rock-cut tombs in Jerusalem until the destruction of the city by the Romans in 70 C.E.

Most of the features that appear in Jason's Tomb remained characteristic of Jewish rock-cut tombs in Jerusalem until the end of the Second Temple period in 70 C.E.: a porch in front of the tomb's entrance, sometimes with two columns *in-antis*; *loculi* cut into the walls of the burial chambers; and a large pyramidal, conical or columnar marker

TODD BOLEN/BIBLEPLACES.COM

constructed over the tomb. In addition, the use of ossuaries replaced the charnel room. Rock-cut tombs with these features surround Jerusalem on the north, east and south. Well-known examples include the Tomb of Bene Hezir in the Kidron Valley, the Tomb of Queen Helena of Adiabene (the so-called Tomb of the Kings) near the American Colony Hotel in East Jerusalem, the Sanhedria tombs (in the modern neighborhood of Sanhedria, in north Jerusalem) and Nicanor's Tomb on Mount Scopus.

When Jesus' body was removed from the cross on the eve of the Jewish Sabbath (Matthew 27:57-59, 28:1; Mark 15:33-34, 42-43; Luke 23:44, 50-54; John 19:31), his followers, all observant Jews, were faced with a problem. Jewish law requires burial within 24 hours (Deuteronomy 21:22), and burials are prohibited on the Sabbath. Therefore Jesus had to be buried before sundown on Friday,

when the Jewish Sabbath begins. Since there was no time to prepare a grave before the beginning of the Sabbath, Joseph of Arimathea placed Jesus' body in his family's rock-cut tomb. The Synoptic Gospels (Matthew, Mark and Luke) are in broad agreement in their description of this event:[5]

Although it was now evening, yet since it was the Preparation Day, that is, the day before the Sabbath, Joseph of Arimathea, a highly respected member of the council, who was himself living in expectation of the reign of God, made bold to go to Pilate and ask for Jesus' body ... And he [Joseph] brought a linen sheet and took him down from the cross and wrapped him in the sheet, and laid him in a tomb that had been hewn out of the rock, and rolled a stone against the doorway of the tomb (Mark 15:42-46).

In the evening a rich man named Joseph of Arimathea, who had himself been a disciple of Jesus, came. He went to Pilate and asked him for Jesus' body ... Then Joseph took the body and wrapped it in a piece of clean linen, and laid it in a new tomb that belonged to him, that he had cut in the rock, and he rolled a great stone over the doorway of the tomb, and went away (Matthew 27:57-60).

Today many scholars believe that since crucifixion was a sadistic and humiliating form of corporal punishment reserved by the Romans for the lower classes (including slaves), Jesus "died a criminal's death on the tree of shame."[6] John Dominic Crossan, for example, argues that Jesus would not have been buried at all, but would have been eaten by dogs. In my opinion, the notion that Jesus was unburied or buried in disgrace is based on a misunderstanding of the archaeological evidence and of Jewish law. Jesus was condemned by the Roman authorities for crimes against Rome, not by the Sanhedrin (Jewish council) for violating Jewish law. The Romans used crucifixion to maintain peace and order and punish rebellious provincials for incitement to rebellion and acts of treason. Although victims of crucifixion were sometimes left on their crosses for days, this was not usually the case.[7] According to the Gospel accounts, Pontius Pilate approved Joseph of Arimathea's request to remove Jesus' body from the cross for burial. Presumably Joseph had to make this special request because he wanted to ensure that Jesus received a proper burial before the beginning of the Sabbath.

After Judea came under direct Roman rule with Pompey's conquest in 63 B.C.E., crucifixion was imposed only by the Roman authorities. Those found guilty by the Sanhedrin of violating Jewish law were executed by stoning (like Jesus' brother James), or were burned, decapitated or strangled: "Four modes of execution were given in the court:

LIKE A HOVERING SPACESHIP, an elegant ceiling rosette decorates a burial chamber in a Second Temple period tomb in Akeldama, south of Jerusalem's Old City. Three *loculi*, or burial niches for the initial burial of the deceased, were carved into the far wall. After the flesh decayed, the bones were placed in ossuaries (bone boxes). The practice of placing bones in an ossuary instead of a rock-cut pit became a common practice from the end of the first century B.C.E. until the Roman destruction of Jerusalem in 70 C.E.

A REPOSITORY was the preferred method of storing the bones of deceased family members until the practice of placing remains in ossuaries arose in the first century B.C.E. Sometimes the rock-carved pits were located directly beneath the rock-carved benches that first held the bodies, as at Ketef Hinnom. After a period of time, the bones would be removed from the bench and placed in the charnel pit, allowing the bench to be reused. A side view (top) shows the charnel pit. Two archaeologists are shown (bottom) peering into the charnel pit at the École Biblique tombs.

RICHARD NOWITZ

WWW.HOLYLANDPHOTOS.ORG

GARO NALBANDIAN

CUT INTO THE ROCK along the Kidron Valley, the tomb of the Bene Hezir family is another example of a rock-hewn tomb with Hellenistic features. Cut out of solid rock, the tomb is decorated with two Doric columns and a carved lintel. The tomb belonged to a wealthy family of priests mentioned in 1 Chronicles 24:15 and Nehemiah 10:20.

stoning, burning, decapitation and strangulation" (Mishnah Sanhedrin 7:1). According to Biblical law (Deuteronomy 21:22), the bodies of executed criminals could be hanged for the purpose of public display only after they were already dead. The hanging of an already executed criminal is described in the Mishnah (the legal corpus of rabbinic Judaism) as follows: "How do they hang him? They drive a post into the ground, and a beam juts out from it, and they tie together his two hands, and thus do they hang him" (Mishnah Sanhedrin 6:4). This passage describes the hands of the deceased being tied together and the body dangling from a pole. In contrast, Roman crucifixion involved spreading apart the arms of a live victim so that he or she could be affixed to the crossbeam by ropes or nails.[8]

The following passage from Josephus indicates that the Jews buried victims of Roman crucifixion in accordance with Jewish law: "Nay, they proceeded to that degree of impiety, as to cast away their bodies without burial, although the Jews used to take so much care of the burial of men, that they took down those that were condemned and crucified, and buried them before the going down of the sun" (*Jewish War* 4.5.2).

The Mishnah attaches no stigma to crucifixion by the Roman authorities and does not prohibit victims of crucifixion from being buried with their families. In contrast, felons who were executed for violating Jewish law could not be buried in family tombs or burial grounds: "And they did not bury [the felon] in the burial grounds of his ancestors. But there were two graveyards made ready for the use of the court, one for those who were beheaded or strangled, and one for those who were stoned or burned" (Mishnah Sanhedrin 6:5).

Only one crucifixion victim—a man named Yehohanan—has ever been discovered and identified by archaeologists.[9] Yehohanan's remains were found in an ossuary in a rock-cut tomb in Jerusalem. According to Crossan, Yehohanan's interment in a rock-cut family tomb is "exceptional and extraordinary" because victims of crucifixion

THE CRUCIFIED ANKLE BONE of a man named Yehohanan is the only archaeological evidence yet found of the Roman practice of crucifixion. Some scholars have claimed that because Jesus was crucified and died a criminal, he would not have received a formal burial in a grave or tomb. Jewish custom, however, permitted the burial in family tombs of those condemned to death by Roman law. The Sanhedrin, the Jewish high court, did not crucify those sentenced to death for violating Jewish law. Therefore, there was nothing about Jesus' death that would have precluded a proper Jewish burial. Yehohanan's ankle bone, found in an ossuary in a rock-cut family tomb in Jerusalem, provides archaeological evidence that crucifixion victims could be buried in a Jewish family tomb.

would not have received an honorable burial.[10] However, as I have just shown, Jewish law does *not* prohibit the burial of victims of crucifixion in family tombs. Crossan argues that "with all those thousands of people crucified around Jerusalem in the first century alone, we have so far found only a single crucified skeleton, and that, of course, preserved in an ossuary. Was burial then, the exception rather than the rule, the extraordinary rather than the ordinary case?"[11]

In my opinion, the exact opposite is the case: The discovery of the identifiable remains of even a single victim of crucifixion is exceptional. Crossan's assumption that we should have the physical (archaeological) remains of additional crucified victims is erroneous for several reasons. First, with one exception (the repository in the late First Temple period cemetery at Ketef Hinnom referred to earlier), not a single undisturbed tomb in Jerusalem has ever been discovered and excavated by archaeologists. This means that even in cases where tombs or ossuaries still contain the original physical remains, the skeletons are often disturbed, damaged or incomplete. Second, the wealthy Jerusalemites who owned rock-cut tombs with ossuaries favored the preservation of the status quo through accommodation with the Romans. Presumably, relatively few of them were executed by crucifixion. Instead, the majority of victims crucified by the Romans belonged to the lower classes—precisely those who could not afford rock-cut tombs. Third, and most important, the nail in Yehohanan's heel was preserved only because of

a fluke. As one authority has observed:

The most dramatic evidence that this young man was crucified was the nail which penetrated his heel bones. But for this nail, we might never have discovered that the young man had died in this way. *The nail was preserved only because it hit a hard knot when it was pounded into the olive wood upright of the cross.* The olive wood knot was so hard that, as the blows on the nail became heavier, the end of the nail bent and curled. We found a bit of the olive wood (between 1 and 2 cm) on the tip of the nail. This wood had probably been forced out of the knot where the curled nail hooked into it. When it came time for the dead victim to be removed from the cross, the executioners could not pull out this nail, bent as it was within the cross. The only way to remove the body was to take an ax or hatchet and amputate the feet.[12]

In other words, the means by which victims were affixed to crosses usually leave no discernable traces in the physical remains or archaeological record. Some victims were bound with ropes, which were untied when the body was removed from the cross. When victims were nailed to a cross, the nails had to be pulled out so that the body could be taken down. This is exactly how the apocryphal *Gospel of Peter* (6:21) describes Jesus' crucifixion: "And then they drew the nails from the hands of the Lord and placed him on the earth." The nail in Yehohanan's ankle, on the other hand, was preserved only because

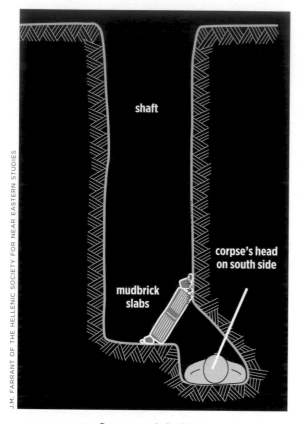

A SHAFT TOMB. Poorer people in the first century C.E., whose families could not afford rock-cut tombs, buried their dead in trench graves. A 5-to-7-foot-deep trench was dug with a niche at the bottom for the body (drawing, above left). The example in the photo above, from Beit Safafa, southwest of Jerusalem, shows two skeletons buried head to toe in the niche at the bottom of the shaft. Other trench graves have been located at Qumran, where the Dead Sea Scrolls were found, and at Khirbet Qazone, southeast of the Dead Sea. Jesus likely would have been buried in such a tomb had Joseph of Arimathea not offered a place in his family's rock-cut tomb.

it bent after hitting a knot in the wood and therefore could not be removed from the body.

Jesus came from a family of modest means that presumably could not afford a rock-cut tomb. Had Joseph of Arimathea not offered Jesus a spot in his family tomb, Jesus likely would have been disposed of in the manner of the poorer classes: in an individual trench grave dug into the ground. This method of burial is similar to the way many dead are buried today. In ancient trench graves, the body of the deceased was wrapped in a shroud and sometimes placed in a wooden coffin. The body was then laid in a hollowed-out space at the base of the trench. After the trench was filled in, a rough headstone

was often erected at one end. The headstones are uninscribed, although some may once have had painted decoration or inscriptions that have not survived. Because trench graves are poor in finds and are much less conspicuous and more susceptible to destruction than rock-cut tombs, relatively few examples are recorded.[13]

In and around Judea examples of trench graves have been found at Qumran, where members of a Jewish sect were buried,[14] at a cemetery near Jerusalem* and in a cemetery near the eastern shore of the Dead Sea.**[15]

When the Gospels tell us that Joseph of Arimathea offered Jesus a spot in his tomb, it is because Jesus' family did not own a rock-cut tomb and there was no time to prepare a grave—that is, there was no time to *dig* a grave, *not* hew a rock-cut tomb—before the Sabbath. It is not surprising that Joseph, who is described as a wealthy Jew, perhaps even a member of the Sanhedrin, had a rock-cut family tomb. The Gospel accounts apparently describe Joseph placing Jesus' body in

*Boaz Zissu, "Odd Tomb Out: Has Jerusalem's Essene Cemetery Been Found?" *Biblical Archaeology Review*, March/April 1999.

**Hershel Shanks, "Who Lies Here? Jordan Tombs Match Those at Qumran," *Biblical Archaeology Review*, September/October 1999.

one of the *loculi* in his family's tomb. The "new" tomb mentioned by Matthew probably refers to a previously unused *loculus*. The Gospels include an accurate description of Jesus' body being wrapped in a linen shroud. When Joseph departed, he sealed the entrance to the tomb by blocking the doorway with a rolling stone.***[16]

Joseph's tomb must have belonged to his family because by definition rock-cut tombs in Jerusalem were family tombs. There is no evidence that the Sanhedrin or the Roman authorities paid for and maintained rock-cut tombs for executed criminals from impoverished families. Instead, these unfortunates would have been buried in individual trench graves or pits. This sort of tradition is preserved in the reference to "the Potter's Field, to bury strangers in" (Matthew 27: 7-8).†

Unlike Crossan, who "cannot find any detailed historical information about the crucifixion of Jesus,"[17] I believe that the Gospel accounts of Jesus' burial are largely consistent with the archaeological evidence. Although archaeology does not prove there was a follower of Jesus named Joseph of Arimathea or that Pontius Pilate granted his request for Jesus' body, the Gospel accounts describing Jesus' removal from the cross and burial are consistent with archaeological evidence and with Jewish law. ▨

***For a discussion of the type of rolling stone that sealed the tomb in which Jesus' body was placed, see Amos Kloner, "Did a Rolling Stone Close Jesus' Tomb?" *Biblical Archaeology Review*, September/October 1999.

†See Leen Ritmeyer and Kathleen Ritmeyer, "Akeldma—Potter's Field or High Priest's Tomb?" *Biblical Archaeology Review*, November/December 1994.

[1] Andrea M. Berlin, "Power and Its Afterlife, Tombs in Hellenistic Palestine," *Near Eastern Archaeology* (*NEA*), June 2002, p. 145.
[2] See Martin Hengel, *Judaism and Hellenism* (Philadelphia: Fortress, 1981), p. 64.
[3] Levy Y. Rahmani, "Jason's Tomb," *Israel Exploration Journal* (*IEJ*) 17, no. 2 (1967), pp. 61-100.
[4] See Nahman Avigad, "Aramaic Inscriptions in the Tomb of Jason," *IEJ* 17, no. 2 (1967), pp. 101-111; Rahmani, "Ancient Jerusalem's Funerary Customs and Tombs, Part Three," *Biblical Archaeologist*, Summer 1981, p. 45.
[5] For a discussion of the differences in the Gospel accounts of this episode, see Byron R. McCane, *Roll Back the Stone, Death and Burial in the World of Jesus* (Harrisburg, PA: Trinity Press International, 2003), pp. 101-102. Here I focus on the accounts of Mark and Matthew, which are generally considered to be earlier and more accurate than Luke. The differences between Mark and Matthew include that Joseph is described as a member of the council/Sanhedrin (Mark) or as a rich man (Matthew) (these two statements are complementary, not contradictory), and Matthew states explicitly that this was Joseph's family tomb, whereas Mark does not (these statements likewise are complementary, not contra-

dictory). Since rock-cut tombs belonged to families, I believe that Matthew is accurate in this detail.
[6] Martin Hengel, *Crucifixion in the Ancient World and the Folly of the Message of the Cross* (Philadelphia: Fortress, 1977), pp. 19, 83, 90. See for example Craig A. Evans, *Jesus and the Ossuaries, What Jewish Burial Practices Reveal about the Beginning of Christianity* (Waco: Baylor University, 2003), p. 101; McCane, *Roll Back the Stone*, p. 89; John Dominic Crossan, *Who Killed Jesus? Exposing the Roots of Anti-Semitism in the Gospel Story of the Death of Jesus* (New York: HarperSanFrancisco, 1995), pp. 160-163; Raymond E. Brown, *The Death of the Messiah from Gethsemane to the Grave: A Commentary on the Passion Narratives in the Four Gospels*, volume two (New York: Doubleday, 1994), p. 947.
[7] McCane, *Roll Back the Stone*, pp. 90, 105; Brown, *The Death of the Messiah*, p. 1207; contra Crossan, *Who Killed Jesus*, pp. 160-161.
[8] The exact manner in which the body was affixed to the cross is debated; for two different reconstructions see Vassilios Tzaferis, "Crucifixion—the Archaeological Evidence," *Biblical Archaeology Review*, January/February 1985; Joseph Zias and Eliezer Sekeles, "The Crucified Man from Giv'at ha-Mivtar: A Reappraisal," *IEJ* 35 (1985), p. 27. Zias and Sekeles note that death resulted from asphyxiation and not from the trauma caused by nailing the body to the cross.
[9] As McCane, *Roll Back the Stone*, pp. 100-101 notes, contrary to Crossan. Also see Tzaferis, "Crucifixion—the Archaeological Evidence"; Rahmani, "Ancient Jerusalem's Funerary Customs," p. 51; Rahmani, *A Catalog of Jewish Ossuaries in the Collections of the State of Israel* (Jerusalem: Israel Antiquities Authority, 1994), p. 131, no. 218. As McCane, *Roll Back the Stone*, p. 99, notes: "Dishonorable burial was reserved for those who had been condemned by *the people of Israel*" (McCane's emphasis). Despite this, McCane concurs that Jesus was buried in shame. The prominence of Yohanan's family is indicated by the fact that another ossuary from this tomb was inscribed "Simon, the builder of the Temple," apparently someone who had participated in the reconstruction of the Temple under Herod; see Tzaferis, "Crucifixion—the Archaeological Evidence," pp. 47, 50; Brown, *The Death of the Messiah from Gethsemane to the Grave*, p. 1210.
[10] Crossan, *Who Killed Jesus*, p. 168; and *The Historical Jesus, The Life of a Mediterranean Peasant* (New York: Harper San Francisco, 1991), p. 391.
[11] See citations in previous note.
[12] Tzaferis, "Crucifixion—the Archaeological Evidence," p. 50; my emphasis. In their reexamination of this skeleton, Zias and Sekeles, "The Crucified Man from Giv'at ha-Mivtar," p. 24, found no evidence for amputation, but confirmed that the nail could not be removed from the heel bone because it was bent: "Once the body was removed from the cross, albeit with some difficulty in removing the right leg, the condemned man's family would now find it impossible to remove the bent nail without completely destroying the heel bone" (p. 27).
[13] See Joseph Patrich, "Graves and Burial Practices in Talmudic Sources," in Itamar Singer, ed., *Graves and Burial Practices in Israel in the Ancient Period* (Jerusalem: Yad Izhak Ben-Zvi, 1994), pp. 191-192 (in Hebrew). In Rome, too, the poor were buried in simple holes dug into the ground; see Jon Davies, *Death, Burial and Rebirth in the Religions of Antiquity* (New York: Routledge, 1999), p. 148. The corpses of paupers and criminals were disposed of in mass graves; see John Bodel, "Graveyards and Groves, A Study of the *Lex Lucerina*," *American Journal of Ancient History* 11 (1994), p. 38.
[14] See Jodi Magness, *The Archaeology of Qumran and the Dead Sea Scrolls* (Grand Rapids, MI: Eerdmans, 2002), pp. 168-175.
[15] Konstantinos D. Politis, "The Nabataean Cemetery at Khirbet Qazone," *NEA*, June 1999, p. 128.
[16] See Brown, *The Death of the Messiah*, pp. 1247-1248.
[17] Crossan, *Who Killed Jesus?*, p. 159; also see his *The Historical Jesus*, p. 393.

Emma

US Where Christ Appeared

Many sites vie for the honor, but Emmaus-Nicopolis is the leading contender

HERSHEL SHANKS

AT DAWN THE TOMB OF JESUS was found empty. Later that very day two of the disciples, Cleopas and another unnamed, were walking on the road to Emmaus when Jesus appeared to them, but they did not recognize him. As they drew near Emmaus, Jesus went to go on, but they pressed him to stay with them, saying, "It is toward evening and the day is now far spent." At dinner, Jesus blessed the bread and gave it to them and "their eyes were opened and they recognized him." All this occurred at a place called Emmaus. That same hour they returned to Jerusalem, where they told the others what had happened. And he appeared to them again! Jesus ate some fish that they gave to him, showing that he had been resurrected bodily. Then he led them out to Bethany on the Mount of Olives, where he blessed them and "was carried up into heaven" (see Luke 24:13–53).

This episode from the Gospel of Luke contains the only mention of Emmaus in the entire New Testament. But Jesus' appearance to his disciples on the road to Emmaus and at dinner is one of only five post-Resurrection appearances recorded in the Gospels.

Where Emmaus was located has been a matter of considerable scholarly controversy. There are at least nine candidates. Only four, however, are serious contenders. Each has three main components that contribute to its possible identification as Emmaus: a spring [Emmaus means "warm

IN THE BREAKING of the bread, two disciples finally recognize the resurrected Jesus in this 1648 painting by Rembrandt van Rijn, titled *The Supper at Emmaus.* (previous pages) Identifying Biblical Emmaus has been difficult because so many sites bear claims to the honored title. The strongest claim, however, now comes from Emmaus-Nicopolis. Recent excavations at the site have turned up a fascinating collection of finds, as well as evidence that it was an important Christian center, drawing pilgrims centuries earlier than the other Emmaus wannabes.

well"], a distance of at least 60 *stadia* (almost 7 miles) from Jerusalem, and a location along a major ancient road. Each also has its problems. How do we decide which one (if any) is the New Testament Emmaus?

Emmaus, or Emmaus-Nicopolis, is the leading contender. Another possibility is Emmaus-Qubeibeh, northwest of Jerusalem (see box on p. 93); an old Roman fort near this site was named *Castellum Emmaus* in the Crusader period. A third contender is Abu Ghosh, just outside of Jerusalem. A spring there may have led some Crusaders to identify it as Emmaus; they built the castle Fontenoide and a church there in 1141. The fourth candidate is Qaloniyeh (ancient Colonia; modern Motza). The Latin for Motza could be *Amassa*; the Greek form, *Ammaous*, mentioned by the turn-of-the-era Jewish historian Josephus, is obviously similar to Emmaus.[1]

The problem with these last three suggestions is that none of them is attested as Emmaus earlier than the Crusader period.

But the first site mentioned, Emmaus-Nicopolis, has its problems too. It is, by the shortest route, about 17 miles from Jerusalem. According to the Gospel of Luke, the disciples "walked" from Jerusalem to Emmaus, ate a meal and then went back to Jerusalem, apparently all in the same day. Is that plausible?

Another problem for Emmaus-Nicopolis concerns the New Testament text. If you look at the Lucan text in your favorite translation, at the first mention of Emmaus it probably says that the village is 7 miles from Jerusalem, or 60 *stadia* in the Greek text from which the translation is taken. If 60 *stadia* is about 7 miles (as it is; a Roman stadium is 607 English feet), then a site at least 17 miles from Jerusalem does not appear to qualify. It's much too far.

So there are two problems with identifying Emmaus-Nicopolis as New Testament Emmaus: First, the disciples would have had to walk about 35 miles in one day. Second, Luke says Emmaus is only 7 miles (60 *stadia*) from Jerusalem.

Consider the second question first: True, if you look at your Bible you will probably find that Luke says Emmaus is 7 miles from Jerusalem. But look at Luke 24:13 in the New Revised Standard Version; there you will find a footnote that says that "other ancient authorities read 160 *stadia*." That figure (approximately 18 miles) fits quite nicely with Emmaus-Nicopolis.

There is plenty of evidence to support both sides of this textual argument—60 versus 160 *stadia*. The often-authoritative fourth-century Codex Sinaiticus says 160 *stadia*. On the other hand, the other two of the great trio of ancient Greek Bibles, Codex Vaticanus and Codex Alexandrinus, both say 60. And each side can assemble a long list of other manuscripts favoring

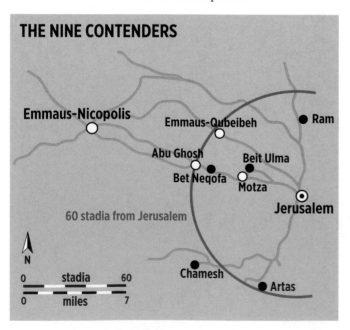

THE NINE CONTENDERS

Emmaus-Nicopolis
Emmaus-Qubeibeh
Ram
Abu Ghosh
Beit Ulma
Bet Neqofa
Motza
Jerusalem
60 stadia from Jerusalem
N
0   stadia   60
0   miles   7
Chamesh
Artas

NINE CONTENDERS for Emmaus lay scattered on ancient roads outside Jerusalem. Each is either (1) historically identified as Emmaus, such as Emmaus-Nicopolis since the fourth century and Emmaus-Quebeibeh and Abu Ghosh since the Crusader period, or (2) their names have vestiges of a Greek word similar to Emmaus, such as Motza. Emmaus-Nicopolis has both the earliest attestation as Emmaus and its Arabic name, Amwas, may preserve its ancient name Emmaus. Many of the sites have springs that led people to assume them to be Emmaus. All are at least 7 miles from Jerusalem and are located along a major ancient road. Emmaus-Nicopolis is by far the farthest from the Holy City, approximately 17 miles away. Could a site that far from Jerusalem be the ancient village of Emmaus?

Another Contender for the Honor: Emmaus-Qubeibeh

The principal competitor of Nicopolis as New Testament Emmaus is el-Qubeibeh, often referred to as Emmaus-Qubeibeh.

The site lies 8 miles northwest of Jerusalem. This fits nicely with 60 *stadia* as the distance between Emmaus and Jerusalem, as specified in most of the ancient copies of the Gospel of Luke. The competitive site of Emmaus-Nicopolis is a viable candidate for New Testament Emmaus only if these ancient witnesses are wrong and the texts that specify 160 stadia are right.

N

12th-century church

Roman (?) house

On the other hand, el-Qubeibeh was never identified as Emmaus until the Crusader period. The earliest reference to the site as Emmaus is in 1290. The suspicion of course is that the Crusaders decided that the site then known only as Qubeibeh was in fact Emmaus because they wanted a spot to point to for pilgrims to the Holy Land—and Qubeibeh fit the distance called for by most copies of the Gospel of Luke. (For the same reason, so the argument goes, some Crusaders also identified Abu Ghosh, just outside of Jerusalem, as Emmaus.)

Scholars who opt for Emmaus-Nicopolis sometimes say that nothing earlier has been found at Emmaus-Qubeibeh. Thus, if true, Qubeibeh was not mentioned as Emmaus until the Crusader period, and nothing has been found at the site earlier than this.

But this is not correct. Qubeibeh was excavated in the early 1940s by Bellarmino Bagatti of the Studium Biblicum Franciscanum. Bagatti describes the site as "a lovely place, marked by shady pines and green olive trees. It gives the impression of an oasis in the midst of the bare tawny hills in which it is located."[1]

The site is dominated by a Crusader period triapsidal church, in one corner of which was an earlier building that may go back to the time of Jesus, according to Bagatti. (Interestingly, the location of this Roman-period house in the northwestern corner of the later church is the same as the Roman house in the church at Emmaus-Nicopolis.) He claims to have found traces of other dwellings that go back as far as the Hellenistic period.

His excavations also unearthed pottery sherds from the Roman period, including a typical Herodian oil lamp, as well as coins securely dated from the third century B.C. to the fifth century A.D. Bagatti concluded there was a village here in the Roman period, although its size could not be determined precisely.

Was this village New Testament Emmaus, as the Crusaders claimed?

[1]Bellarmino Bagatti, *Emmaus-Qubeibeh*, translated by Raphael Bonanno (Jerusalem: Franciscan Printing Press, 1993), p. X.

it, although the list containing 60 *stadia* is longer. On the other hand, Eusebius (third–fourth-century author of the famous *Onomasticon*), Jerome (fourth-century church father and translator of the Bible and the *Onomasticon* into Latin), Origen (third-century church father) and Sozomen (fifth-century church historian) all opt for 160 *stadia* as the correct Lucan text, thus supporting Emmaus-Nicopolis as the best candidate for New Testament Emmaus. Emmaus-Nicopolis is assumed to be the site of the Lucan Emmaus by almost all Christian pilgrim texts from the fourth century onward.

Modern scholars are just as divided as the ancient sources. According to *Eerdman's Dictionary of the Bible*, "None [of the leading candidates for Biblical Emmaus] has won widespread approval." The *Anchor Bible Dictionary* says 60 *stadia* is "the better reading." The Editorial Committee of the United Bible Societies' Greek New Testament

calls the reading of 160 *stadia* a "scribal blunder," the result of patristic efforts to confirm the site of Nicopolis as Biblical Emmaus. On the other hand, three prominent Israeli scholars in their recent *Tabula Imperii Romani Judaea-Palaestina* tell us that New Testament Emmaus is "probably Emmaus-Nicopolis."[2]

What about the first problem? Is it reasonable to think that the disciples could walk more than 35 miles in a day? Here again, scholars are divided: The distance makes the reading of 160 *stadia*, according to the *Anchor Bible Dictionary*, "surely wrong"; people could not walk 35 miles in a day. On the other hand, "Anyone familiar with Palestinian Bedouin or Arabs in a pre-automotive culture would not doubt the disciples' ability to walk forty miles in a day," says the *HarperCollins Bible Dictionary*.

Someone recently identified another problem: The disciples arrived at Emmaus when it was "toward evening and the day ... far spent" (Luke 24:29). Would the disciples have eaten and then departed for Jerusalem after dark? No. In the orient, evening begins at 12 o'clock noon, when the sun begins to go down. They would have left in the early afternoon. Once they had finished their meal, they would have departed immediately to spread the good news. Moreover, although the

"I BAPTIZE WITH WATER." The Byzantine trefoil baptismal font at Emmaus is one of the best preserved in the Holy Land. Two steps lead down into the basin where the penitent would stand when the priest poured water over him (the basin is not large enough for total immersion). Only a bishopric seat would have a baptismal font in a separate building, rather than as part of the church, which gives further evidence of the importance of Emmaus in the Byzantine period.

GARO NALBANDIAN

EMMAUS'S MAIN CHURCH was built up over the centuries. Excavators believe that the earliest stratum is Herodian and may include remnants of a house that came to be revered as the "Cleopas House," where Jesus broke bread and was recognized by his disciples after the Resurrection. A Byzantine triapsidal basilica was built over the Roman remains. Sources as early as Eusebius and Jerome considered this village to be the actual site of Jesus' appearance. The Crusaders built a church upon the old Byzantine remains, and its walls can still be seen today.

THE THREE CHURCHES at Emmaus were explored in the 1920s by Dominican priest Louis-Hugues Vincent. His drawing depicts his findings with the dates he considered accurate. The large southern basilica (black lines) he dated prior to 529. The smaller, northern church (blue) he considered to be of a later construction. The Crusader church (12th century, red) was built upon the remains of the Byzantine basilica, which in turn was built over the remnants of a Roman house (green). The current excavators now date the northern church prior to 430 because they found a mosaic decorated with crosses (which were banned by Emperor Theodosius that year) and a coin from the reign of Emperor Elagabalus (218–222 A.D.).

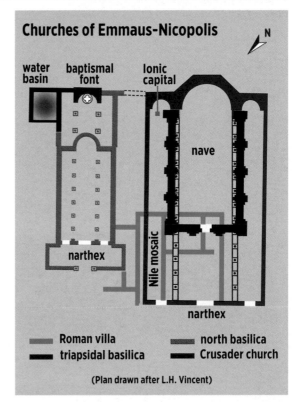

Churches of Emmaus-Nicopolis

(Plan drawn after L.H. Vincent)

text does not specify this, it is possible that they took a donkey or even ran part of the way out of sheer excitement in order to complete their trip to Jerusalem as quickly as possible and tell the other disciples of the appearance of the risen Lord.

In modern times Emmaus-Nicopolis was identified as New Testament Emmaus by the American Orientalist Edward Robinson when he canvassed the Holy Land in the mid-19th century.

Robinson identified hundreds of Biblical sites, often on the basis of the survival of the Biblical name in current Arabic names. For example, the Arabic place-name Seilun identified Shiloh; Beitun identified Bethel; and Amwas ('Imwas), the Arab village at the site of Emmaus-Nicopolis, identified Emmaus. It occupies a strategic position near

FOUND NEAR A ROMAN GRAVE this Egyptian scarab from the 20th to 19th centuries B.C. depicts a "fighting god," his fists clenched. Under his left arm is a uraeus—the typical snake symbol of ancient Egyptian kings. How did this Egyptian scarab find its way to Emmaus? It may have been a talisman of the family buried in the grave, or there may be more ancient remains from the Early to Middle Bronze Age hiding deeper down in the strata of Emmaus.

Latrun, on the ancient road from the coast up to Jerusalem.

South of the village, Robinson also found the remains of an old church constructed of long, well-cut stones, with a semi-circular apse still standing at the end. In 1879 a French architect named Joseph Guillemot conducted the first archaeological excavation at the site and found, in the north apse of what was originally a triapsidal church, a pseudo-Ionic capital inscribed on one side, "One God," and on the other, "Blessed be his name forever" (cf. Psalm 72:19). The first side is in Greek, the other side in what was thought to be Hebrew but is now identified by Israeli scholar Leah di Segni as Samaritan. At first the two inscriptions seemed to be from two different eras, but it is more likely that the capital dates to the fifth or sixth century A.D. The first side of the inscription ("God is one") may be, the current excavators suggest, an echo of Deuteronomy 6:4: "Hear, O Israel, the Lord our God, the Lord is one." The second inscription testifies to the presence of Samaritans (as well as Jews, Christians and Romans) in Emmaus. In any event,

as subsequent Christian finds seem to make clear, the locals identified the site early on as the place of Jesus' post-Resurrection appearance.[3]

Between 1924 and 1930, Louis-Hugues Vincent, a prominent Dominican priest at the École Biblique et Archéologique Française in Jerusalem, excavated this church. In one corner of the nave, he found what he regarded as the remains of an earlier domestic structure that he dated to the Roman period. It was built of

"ONE GOD, blessed be his name forever" is inscribed on this fifth–sixth-century A.D. pseudo-Ionic capital, which was discovered in 1879. The first part, on one side, is in Greek (above left); the second part is in Samaritan script (bottom left). Some scholars believe the first side to be a reflection of Deuteronomy 6:4, "Hear O Israel, the Lord our God, the Lord is one," and the second side to be a reflection of Psalm 72:19, "And blessed be his glorious name forever."

Herodian ashlars, and even earlier Hasmonean coins were found there. Perhaps the church was purposely built atop this house because it was thought to be "Cleopas's House," where the disciples recognized the resurrected Jesus. Perhaps this belief occasioned the construction of the church above the house. The new excavation team (see below) thinks the site may have been a *domus ecclesia*, a place of Christian worship before Constantine's time (early fourth century). They also suggest that a fourth-century Byzantine chapel may have been erected on the site prior to the subsequent building of the triapsidal basilical church in the fifth century.

North of the church—and associated with it— Vincent identified an impressive structure as a baptistery.[5] Within the baptistery is a beautiful trefoil baptismal font, one of the best-preserved baptismal fonts in the Holy Land (see photo, p. 94). The baptistery building was supported by four columns. One of the column bases of the baptistery is still *in situ*. During this early period, only at bishopric seats were baptisteries in separate structures. This architectural feature is another indication of the city's importance to Byzantine Christians.

In front of the baptistery, Father Vincent also excavated another church, which lies just north of the remains of the triapsidal church (see plan, p. 95). Within the triapsidal church, he also explored a third church, which he attributed to the Crusader period (12th century). Although the precise dates for these structures are disputed, it appears clear that, at a very early period, the site was thought to be Emmaus of the New Testament and became an important center of Christian worship and pilgrimage. It is uncertain whether the site's Christian importance resulted from its association with New Testament Emmaus or, on the other hand, a manufactured association led to the site's Christian importance. This remains a question that can never be answered definitively.

More than 25 years ago, the current director of German archaeological work in the Holy Land, Karl-Heinz Fleckenstein, and his wife, Louisa, were guiding tours of Christian sites and became fascinated with Emmaus-Nicopolis. At that time, the site was abandoned and neglected. The Fleckensteins decided to try to mount an archaeological expedition to uncover new evidence for the correct identification of the site and the dates of many of its structures. The excavation, which

A HEBREW MEMORIAL was found in Abu Kabir, near Jaffa, that mentions the city of Emmaus in an epitaph for "Eleazar, the son of Yehoshua. Peace from Emmaus. Peace." The inscribed stone tablet dates to the Roman-Byzantine period when it was common to mention one's birthplace in an epitaph. Eleazar was clearly proud of the city from which he had come.

PAVEL SHRAGO/THE OLD JAFFA MUSEUM OF ANTIQUITIES

GARO NALBANDIAN

"IN THE NAME OF THE FATHER and the Son and the Holy Spirit, Beautiful is the city of the Christians" reads this Byzantine-period stone tablet. It was found in 1894 on a ridge west of the Arab village of Amwas (Emmaus-Nicopolis), where excavators believe they have uncovered ancient Emmaus. The plaque indicates that the city was predominantly Christian in the Byzantine period.

finally began in 1993 and continued until 2005, was sponsored by a consortium of institutions including the Studium Biblicum Franciscanum in Jerusalem, represented by the well-known scholar Father Michele Piccirillo. The Fleckensteins and archaeologist Mikko Louhivuori served as

GARO NALBANDIAN

principal investigators. Since 2005 the excavators have been studying the finds and preparing an excavation report, but they also hope to return to the field.

The Fleckensteins believe that the site was identified as New Testament Emmaus as early as the third century. Of course, the later a contending site was identified as Emmaus, the less likely it is to be Emmaus of the New Testament. The oldest identification of Emmaus-Nicopolis does seem to go back much further than that of any of the other contenders.

In 130 A.D. an earthquake destroyed much of the site. For nearly a century thereafter, it was little more than a small village. One of the villagers, however, became prominent and influential: Sextus Julius Africanus was a Christian historian, traveler and Roman prefect. Africanus wrote a five-volume history of the world from the Creation to 221 A.D. (the *Chronografiai*). The well-known Church father Origen called Africanus his "brother in God through Jesus Christ." In 222 Africanus led a delegation to Rome to seek the

designation of *polis* for his city. The petition was granted by the emperor Elagabalus, and the city was named Emmaus-Nicopolis, the "victorious city of Emmaus." As Emmaus-Nicopolis, the city began to thrive once again.

One never knows what one will find in an archaeological excavation. That is part of what makes it so exciting—and mysterious. Certainly one of the most unexpected finds at Emmaus was an Egyptian scarab of the Hyksos type (see photo, p. 96). It depicts a masculine figure wearing a tall, cylindrical head cover. His hands are in the position of a "fighting god" with clenched fists. Under his left fist is a *uraeus* (serpent), the symbol of ancient Egyptian kings.[6] The scarab dates to about 1800 B.C. What in the world was it doing at Emmaus? It was found near a Roman grave and may have been a talisman passed down through the generations. Or perhaps there was an Egyptian city here in the Middle Bronze Age, a city that still lies buried deep underground, awaiting discovery by another team of archaeologists. A grave from this period is said to

MANY MOSAICS have been found at Emmaus-Nicopolis—most from the Byzantine period. Flora and fauna graced the floor of the northern nave of the fifth-century Byzantine church. Two birds sit peacefully in a papyrus plant (opposite). More sinister happenings occur in other panels of the floor; a lion stalks his prey; a gazelle loses its life to a hungry leopard (right). The excavators call it the "Nile Mosaic" and see it as representing the fight between Good and Evil.

GARO NALBANDIAN

have been found in nearby Neve Shalom. In the meantime, Middle Bronze specialists must now consider the significance of an Egyptian scarab found at Emmaus-Nicopolis.[7]

Most of the archaeological evidence uncovered here, however, comes from the Byzantine period but includes evidence from Hellenistic and Roman periods as well.

Jews, Samaritans, Romans and, later, Christians all lived here in what must have been a major town.

In the city museum of Jaffa, just south of Tel Aviv, is a fragmentary inscription from a Jewish tombstone that reads in Hebrew: "This is the resting place of Eleazar, son of Yehoshua. Peace from Emmaus. Peace." According to Shimshon Seder, director of the museum, the tombstone was found in Abu Kabir (between Tel Aviv and Jaffa), about 17 miles from Emmaus-Nicopolis, and dates to the Roman-Byzantine era. Apparently this Eleazar hailed from Emmaus, most likely Emmaus-Nicopolis, which is closer to the find-spot than any of the other contenders. Eleazar was doubtless proud of coming from such an important town, and it was the custom at the time to indicate one's hometown in an epitaph. This inscription is further evidence of the probable early identification of the site as New Testament Emmaus and is important for the epigraphic evidence of Emmaus written in Hebrew script.[8]

By the Byzantine period, the evidence suggests that Emmaus had become a fully Christian city. In 1894 a shattered stone plaque was discovered on a ridge to the west, overlooking Emmaus. The plaque, which cannot date epigraphically before the fourth century A.D., is now in the museum of the White Fathers adjacent to the Church of St. Anne in Jerusalem and reads in Greek: "In the name of the Father and the Son and the Holy Spirit, beautiful is the city of the Christians."

Since this inscription was found overlooking Emmaus, it is likely that it came from there. It may have stood over the portal of a church.[9]

The remains of the fifth-century Byzantine basilica (the south church) were overbuilt by the Crusader church, which still dominates the site. In the narthex area of the basilica (in front of the nave), the excavation team uncovered a graceful sixth-century A.D. mosaic featuring a chalice overflowing with water from which two birds are drinking. It is not difficult to imagine a variety of symbolic interpretations. The mosaic also includes fragments of fish, a bull, the head of a lamb, and other animals. In the middle is an inscription reading *Kyrie Eleison* ("Lord, Have Mercy") and the genitive (possessive) form of the name Titus.

Beneath a mosaic in the south church, the excavators found a line of eight skeletons, all facing east toward the rising sun (as do churches from this period), with their arms crossed over their chests in Christian penitence, perhaps representing the cross. A radiocarbon test performed by the Weizmann Institute in Rehovot, Israel, indicates that the bones date somewhere between 260 and 420 A.D. They are probably the bones of monks who served in the church and who were buried without grave goods.

Another mosaic, found in the nave of the south church (where Vincent identified the

JEWISH PRESENCE at Emmaus is evident in the rock-cut graves from the Herodian period that employed typical Jewish burial practices. The deceased was first placed in a niche (*loculus* in English, *kokh* in Hebrew) in the cave wall deep enough to hold the body. Three of these niches can be seen in this picture. The stone at the left of the picture above appears to be a device with which to block the door. After a year, when the flesh had fallen away, the deceased's bones were placed in a limestone bone box, or ossuary. The close-up at right shows typical decoration on Jewish ossuaries of the time.

Roman house), resembles the "Nile" scenes popular in the Byzantine period (see photos on pp. 98–99). In one panel a leopard attacks a gazelle; in another a lion takes down his prey. These representations of the danger of the wild contrast with nearby scenes of birds nestled peacefully in papyrus plants. These contradictory images are a common motif used by early Christian artists, sometimes said to symbolize the fight between Good and Evil. In his interpretation, Fleckenstein sees a reflection of the glorious appearance of the risen Jesus to his disciples in Emmaus after the "bloody and cruel events on Golgatha."[10]

The excavators have uncovered a wide range of Christian artifacts, unfortunately often of uncertain date but mainly of the Byzantine period. For example, one of the hundreds of clay oil lamps from the Byzantine period (fourth–seventh centuries) is inscribed: "May the light of Christ shine on everyone" (cf. John 1:9). Others were decorated with depictions of ladders that perhaps symbolize the steps down into a baptismal font. These lamps are probably to be associated with the baptistery mentioned earlier.

The site is peppered with tombs of various kinds from many different periods. A number of them have recently been excavated.

One of the tombs revealed clear evidence of a Jewish presence in Jesus' time: four ossuaries. Limestone bone boxes called ossuaries were used by Jews for secondary burial of bones, only from about 20 B.C. to 70 A.D. Thousands of ossuaries have been found in the Jerusalem area. The deceased was initially laid to rest on a stone bench in a cave or in a long rock cavity called a *koch* in Hebrew (plural, *kochim*) and a *loculus* in English (plural, *loculi*). About a year later, after the flesh had desiccated and fallen away, the bones were placed in an ossuary. Near the burial cave with these ossuaries were two rolling stones, presumably used to close tombs, much like those that must have closed Jesus' tomb in Jerusalem.

But these were only partially cut. Parts of the stones were still attached to the bedrock, as if the stone cutter had stopped for the day, intending to return to work in the morning.

Of the thousands of coins the excavators recovered, one is especially interesting: a coin of Valerius Gratus (15–26 A.D.). He was the Roman procurator who preceded Pontius Pilate. Gratus restructured the Temple governance in Jerusalem and appointed first Annas and then Caiaphas as High Priests.

We have emphasized the Christian connections with Emmaus. But, in addition to Jews and Samaritans, the city boasted an important Roman population. Indeed, probably the most elegant structure in the ancient city was a Roman villa that was found northwest of the basilicas and is being excavated by the current team. This villa had a mosaic floor and what appears to be the remains of a dye industry. Three basins carved into the rock permitted the passage of liquids from one basin to the other. A coin from the reign of Emperor Elagabalus (218–222 A.D.) was found, providing a probable date for the structure. As for the occupants, only a comb was found that might be connected to the lady of the house.

The continuing excavation of the site promises to shed new light on the intriguing history of Emmaus-Nicopolis. 🔲

Kathleen E. Miller provided research, reporting and translation of the German for this article.

THE STONE WAS ROLLED AWAY. The burial caves from the Herodian period were often closed with a rolling stone to keep people and animals from entering the tomb, but the stone could also be moved aside when the time came for family to enter. This rolling stone from Emmaus-Nicopolis found in front of one of the caves is only partially cut, as if the stone mason had finished work for the day, but then never returned.

[1] Vincent Michel, "Emmaus in Lukas 24,13: Traditionsentwicklung und Textkritik." In Karl-Heinz Fleckenstein, Mikko Louhivouri and Rainer Riesner, *Emmaus in Judäa: Geschichte-Exegese-Archäologie* (Basel: Brunnen, 2003), pp. 122–141.

[2] S.v. "Colonia, Emmaus, Moza," Yoram Tsafrir, Leah Di Segni and Judith Green, *Tabula Imperii Romani Judaea-Palaestina* (Jerusalem: Israel Academy of Sciences and Humanities, 1994), p. 105. This entry has a very extensive bibliography.

[3] Fleckenstein, "Zur Geschichte der Erforschung von Emmaus/Nikopolis," in Fleckenstein et al., *Emmaus in Judäa*, pp. 219 and 286–289.

[4] Michael Avi-Yonah, "Emmaus," in Ephraim Stern and Ayelet Lewinson-Gilboa, eds., *New Encyclopedia of Excavations in the Holy Land*, Vol. 2 (New York: Simon & Schuster, 1993), pp. 385–387.

[5] Avi-Yonah, "Emmaus."

[6] Alviero Niccacci, "Der Skarabäus von Amwas," in Fleckenstein et al., *Emmaus in Judäa*, pp. 297–298.

[7] Fleckenstein, "Inschriften and Münzen aus Emmaus/Nikopolis," in *Emmaus in Judäa*, pp. 279–280.

[8] Fleckenstein, "Inschriften and Münzen aus Emmaus/Nikopolis," in Fleckenstein et al., *Emmaus in Judäa*, pp. 284–285.

[9] Fleckenstein, "Inschriften and Münzen aus Emmaus/Nikopolis," in Fleckenstein et al., *Emmaus in Judäa*, pp. 293–294.

[10] Fleckenstein, "Das Nilus-Mosaik—Versuch einer Interpretation," in Fleckenstein et al., *Emmaus in Judäa*, pp. 274–278.

Jesus OF Jesus HISTORY VS. Jesus OF Jesus TRADITION

BAR INTERVIEWS SEAN FREYNE

Sean Freyne was the director of Mediterranean and Near Eastern Studies, as well as an Emeritus Professor of Theology, at Trinity College Dublin. His research focused on the integration of literary and archaeological sources for understanding the social and religious world of Galilee in Hellenistic and Roman times. Editor Hershel Shanks sat down with Professor Freyne in New Orleans to discuss what archaeology and Biblical studies can tell us about the historical Jesus.

HERSHEL SHANKS: Sean, I take it you've come to New Orleans for the annual meeting of the Society of Biblical Literature [SBL]?

SEAN FREYNE: That's true, Hershel, but also I'm retracing my footsteps of 30 years ago and more, when I taught here in New Orleans at Loyola University. My first daughter, Bridget, was born here. So I have very special memories of New Orleans.

I'm glad to be able to talk to you. My only fear is that our typist won't be able to understand your thick Irish brogue.
No, no, I speak very clearly. I speak slowly and clearly in my best Americanese. [laughter]

You're a senior scholar. What do you get out of these meetings of the Society of Biblical Literature?
Well, I found coming to the SBL was a very stimulating experience even as a young scholar. I had been trained in Europe, of course, in Rome and Jerusalem and then subsequently in Germany. And when I came to teach in the States, I found that the discipline [of Biblical studies] here was different from Europe. While I don't always agree with everything I hear from the United States in the field of Biblical studies, nonetheless I always find it very challenging and very stimulating. And so I see myself as kind of bridging a European, more theological, approach with a more secular one, particularly in regard to historical Jesus studies. In

ERICH LESSING

ARCHAEOLOGY OF THE GALILEE has been invaluable for fleshing out the Jewish context of the historical Jesus, according to theologian and archaeologist Sean Freyne. In his interview with *Biblical Archaeology Review* editor Hershel Shanks, Freyne discusses how historical Jesus studies attempt to shed light on the figure behind the gospel narratives and the early Jesus movement.

America there is a greater emphasis on sociological methods, which can be very helpful, but which also can be quite restrictive.

You are an expert in historical Jesus studies. I have always wondered about that name. Are there nonhistorical Jesus studies, or unhistorical Jesus studies?
[Laughing] That's a good question. Some people confuse the notion of the historical Jesus with the notion of the actual or the real Jesus. I think the historical Jesus is a construct, a theological construct, really. It's the figure of Jesus as he is represented in the documents of Christian faith as a historical person.

I thought it was just the opposite, that the historical Jesus was opposed to the theological Jesus.
What we're trying to do, I think, in this quest for the historical Jesus is to find the figure who stands behind the gospel narratives as a historical figure. If we look at the Gospels, all we have, in the case of the Synoptics [Matthew, Mark and Luke], is one year of his public ministry. If we include John, we make it three years. It's a bird's-eye view of this figure who walked the roads of Galilee. We have no record whatever of Jesus' early life. We have the infancy gospel stories, which of course are highly theological and highly literary, made up later. So we really can't build anything historical on those narratives.

In Hebrew Bible studies, there's a big question about whether Solomon and David lived. Archaeologists have now found an inscription that actually refers to David's dynasty. So that's settled. But Solomon is still an open question and of course there is no archaeological evidence of Moses. Yet you never hear about historical Moses studies or historical Solomon studies or even historical David studies. Why the contrast? You have it only with Jesus.
Someone has said that if Moses didn't exist, we'd have to invent him. He stands behind a whole tradition. We

know very little about him. So little in fact, that as an historical person he is virtually lost to history too. But I think the Israelite tradition as it developed, as well as later Jewish tradition, weren't as dependent on one figure as the Christian tradition was on this figure of Jesus of Nazareth. I think that's why the historical Jesus becomes a real battleground theologically and historically, because so much is at stake in terms of the Christian proclamation.

If we say Jesus is purely a construct, without any historical roots, then Christianity itself would be in danger of collapsing. The same is true for the traditions of Israelite origin. If we can't somehow put some trust in the early traditions—the legal traditions, the Exodus tradition, the origins in Egypt and so on—if we can't put some trust in those, then it seems to me the whole story, as a religious expression, would be in danger of collapsing also.

So I think, in other words, something of the historical roots of the tradition, both the Israelite tradition and the early Christian tradition, are important for the kind of theological religious claims that are invested in those figures and those histories. But I think we have to recognize that our ancient sources cannot be judged by the standards of modern historiography. We have to try to work with historical methods and try at the same time to recognize the literary creations, be it about Jesus or about Israel.

I thought there was a more intense debate and acrimony among those who are arguing over whether there was a United Monarchy ruled by David and Solomon than there is in New Testament studies about the historical Jesus.
No, no. There is quite an intense debate in the historical Jesus studies as well.

Some New Testament scholars say Jesus was a magician.
They use that term. But a lot depends on how you use the word

"magician". Is it a pejorative term? Some people have said Jesus was a shaman, others say he was a Hasid [a very religious Jew]. We have a whole range of images of Jesus floating around. "Magician" is used as a way of discrediting somebody in antiquity. According to Celsus [a second-century C.E. Greek philosopher], Jesus went to Egypt and learned magic there, and came back and deceived the people. I think we have to try to balance a negative account with what we can establish historically. And I think that "magician," for me, is not the appropriate title.

Another characterization of Jesus is as a Greek-style philosopher, who is a Cynic.
Yes. The Cynics were traveling popular philosophers that were to some degree counter-cultural figures. When some scholars say that Jesus was a Cynic, there is often the implication that he wasn't Jewish, or only marginally so, since the Cynics were a phenomenon of the Greco-Roman urban environment. That is where I think the archaeology of Galilee can help. When I wrote my first book on Galilee, I came across a book published in German in 1941 by Walter Grundmann, a professor of New Testament. The title was *Jesus der Galiläer—Jesus the Galilean*—which claimed that because Galilee in Jesus' time was heathen, with great probability, "*Jesus kein Jude war*," "Jesus was not a Jew." Although it was published in Germany in 1941 at the height of the Nazi period, there had been that scholarly tradition going back to the 19th century, and to some extent it is still with us, as in the Cynic Jesus hypothesis: The Greek world was enlightened; the Jewish world, the Semitic world, was backward and outdated. In a sense, making Jesus Greek was a way of saying Jesus is not tied to the particularities of his Jewish tradition. It was making him a figure of universal significance—that was the dominant trend of 19th-century Jesus studies.

A MODEST DWELLING recently excavated in the heart of modern Nazareth is the first residential structure from the time of Jesus to be discovered at the site. The building consists of two rooms and a courtyard and contained fragments of Early Roman pottery (first–second century C.E.) and stone vessels that were used by Jews because they didn't become ritually unclean, as pottery vessels do. Freyne believes that Jesus was most likely born in the same small Galilee village of Nazareth where he grew up. His family may have had ties to Judea, however, and the gospel writers may have made Bethlehem in Judea the location of the nativity as a theological construct linking Jesus with the messianic line and house of David.

You seem to be saying that Galilee was Jewish but absorbed Hellenistic culture at the time of Jesus and yet was not overcome or overrun by it.

It didn't lose its distinctive Jewish identity. In the interior of Galilee, for instance, you do not find any of the things that we associate with a Greek or Roman city in terms of monumental buildings or statues of the gods.

Has archaeology helped to counter that view?

Absolutely, very clearly.

How?

In a number of ways. First and foremost it has shown that the reception of Greek influences in the Near East from the time of Alexander the Great [fourth century B.C.E.] was not a hostile clash of civilizations, as has often been asserted. The question is at what point, or to what extent, were the unique claims of the Jewish tradition, for instance that of Yahweh as the only God, abandoned in favor of a polytheistic understanding of the divine? Archaeology has shown that the Jewish identity maintained itself despite the dangers of total assimilation, but Jews also benefited from the advantages of the Greek world. The Jewish diaspora was Greek, and the

Hebrew Scriptures were translated into Greek in the third century B.C.E. already. Philo of Alexandria, one of the great Jewish philosophers, was heavily influenced by Greek philosophy in first-century C.E. Alexandria. So Greek culture was not necessarily hostile to the Jewish tradition, which came under the impact of Hellenism in various ways. But it also vigorously resisted abandoning its own distinctive worldview. It accommodated itself to Hellenism while at the same time it retained its own distinctive identity. That, to me, is crucial to the understanding of Jesus also.

Archaeology, I think, has shown us that there was indeed a strong element of Hellenization in terms of trade, language, military and administrative strategies, etc. It was to some extent a case of acting Greek without becoming Greek, as somebody has put it.

You feel that Jesus was imbued with Jewish culture?

Absolutely. To my mind there's no question about that. Locating him more precisely within that culture is another question. Jewish culture at the time was not monochromic. There were different varieties of Judaism—diaspora, or Greek-speaking Jews, the Sadducees, proto-rabbinic Jews such as the Essenes and the Pharisaic movement, etc. Where we locate the Jesus movement in this matrix is the big question historically.

What are the alternatives?

Well, for me, one of the important things is to start with Jesus' relationship with John the Baptist. We know from John's gospel that, later, the Jesus and the Baptist movements were in opposition, since their disciples were in competition for members (John

TODD BOLEN/WWW.BIBLEPLACES.COM

it as one movement among various strands in Judaism that are beginning to be disaffected, not just politically but religiously. Herod changed the high priesthood. He got rid of the Hasmoneans [the previous Jewish rulers] and brought in replacement high priests from outside, from Egypt and from Mesopotamia.

I think we can see some disaffection here; the symbolic system of the Temple was not functioning as well as it might have in terms of being the religious center for the whole people. Luke presents the Baptist as the son of a country priest (Luke 1:5–8). Now, if John's the son of a country priest, what's he doing in the desert, preaching forgiveness of sins? He should be in Jerusalem talking about how people should come there on Yom Kippur. Instead, he's undermining the system that is functioning in Jerusalem, just as the Qumran people [where the Dead Sea Scrolls were found] are as well, by claiming that they are an alternative temple. We have to see that kind of movement in the first century in this larger context. I would want to locate Jesus as well within that general environment.

3:26). In this gospel the Baptist is apologetically presented as being the first witness to the Christian gospel (John 1:29–34). In the much-earlier synoptic account, Jesus says that "nobody born of women is greater than John the Baptist" (Matthew 11:11;

Luke 7:28). These are the words of an admirer of John. Jesus has left his Galilean village culture of Nazareth and joins the Baptist movement in the desert, it would seem.

Now how do we understand the Baptist movement in the desert? I see

Z. RADOVAN/WWW.BIBLELANDPICTURES.COM

Where within that context?

All the Gospels say that once John was arrested, Jesus moved into Galilee. Now that move is very important. He's going back to Galilee, going back to his own roots, but he's not going back to settle in Nazareth.

There's a famous story in Mark where Jesus is in a house with people gathered around him, and they say to him, "Your mother and brothers are outside waiting for you and calling for you [Mark 3:32]." Mark had made a very unexpected assertion that [his family] thought that Jesus was out of his mind [Mark 3:21–22]. But Jesus does not go out to meet them. Instead he makes this amazing statement, asking "Who are my mother and my brothers?" Those who do the will of my father, he says, are my brothers and sisters and mother [Mark 3:33–35]. In other words, he's establishing a new kind of family that is based not on kinship, but on following his way of understanding what God's will is. For me, those are some of the core moments in trying to reconstruct the way I see Jesus developing a new vision within the contemporary varieties of Judaism in Galilee.

The prophet Isaiah was very important for Jesus, as he was for all these renewal movements, including the people at Qumran. The remains of several different Isaiah scrolls have been found in the caves there, including one complete scroll and another nearly complete.

In Isaiah you have a clear sense

of the remaking of Israel after the Babylonian Exile and the hopes that that engendered. The servant figure will bring light to the nations as well as restore Israel. There's a sense of the universal in Isaiah. I tend to see John the Baptist more focused on Israel, and Jesus as adopting a more open and inclusive approach to renewal. They are both building their visions of what Israel's role is, even when the emphasis is different. The Jesus movement is thus a renewal group built around the figure of the servant of God, as depicted in Isaiah, who is not militantly opposed to foreigners. Yet he addresses his message to Israel. The servant figure is deeply embedded in a tradition of Jewish piety associated with the *anavim* or "pious poor" whom we meet in the Prophets and Psalms [Isaiah 3:14–15; Ezekiel 18:12; Psalms 9:13, 10:12, 25:9, 34:3]. They are often depicted in Isaiah as suffering at the hands of the ruling elite associated with the temple, yet especially dear to God (Isaiah 58:1–14, 61:1–3, 65:13–14).

Did Jesus initiate his own unique renewal movement or was he part of another renewal movement?

I think Jesus began within the renewal movement that was associated with the desert and with John the Baptist, as I have been saying. And then his strategy changes from John's. John's world vision is of an imminent judgment, that God is going to come and separate the good

from the wicked, a highly apocalyptic worldview. He remains in the desert summoning people to come out and prepare themselves through repentance and baptism. Jesus seems to be less influenced by the apocalyptic view of history. He retains it, but he's not as influenced by it. So when he goes into Galilee, he attempts to wed the apocalyptic worldview with a "wisdom" one, as he moves around the villages preaching and healing In other words, he recognizes that this world is essentially good. You can examine many of his parables, for example, where he talks about nature reflecting God's ways with the world, as in the parables of growth [Mark 4]: seeds falling into different kinds of soil. It's not a vision of God coming in thunder and lightning. God is in the world already. So I think Jesus operates out of what I would call a creation tradition, where true wisdom is about understanding the ways of the world and recognizing God's active presence in its processes. I think Jesus puts more emphasis on the wisdom tradition than the purely apocalyptic one. In that sense he is less a John the Baptist figure, more a prophetic one who is able to extend his calling not merely to Israel but to the nations also, accepting that the nations, too, can share with Israel's blessings.

Was this unique to Jesus or was this part of another Jewish movement?

That was already in Isaiah. In Isaiah 49:6 [in so-called Deutero-Isaiah or Second Isaiah], for example. Yahweh [Israel's God] is addressing the servant. "It is too little a thing," he says, "for you to restore the tribes of Israel. You must be a light for the nations that my salvation may reach to the ends of the earth." So the servant figure, when Israel is restored, will be a light unto the nations. That is Isaiah's vision of "all peoples" coming from the various points of the compass to the great banquet described in Isaiah 25:6. In the latter part of the book (Trito-Isaiah, i.e., Isaiah 56–66), this same universal perspective is retained alongside the special role of Israel—long before Jesus.

Was Jesus alone in this, or was he part of a larger Jewish movement?

The Isaiah tradition kept being reworked in one way or another. We see it in the Book of Daniel, as well as in 1 Enoch and in the Testament of the Twelve Patriarchs [both in the Apocrypha]. There's a lot of reworking of the tradition going on. We have no evidence, however, of another movement quite like the Jesus movement. I use the term "Jesus movement" because it's very difficult to distinguish between Jesus as a historical figure and the movement that emerges in his name in Galilee. I think that Jesus' first followers continued to imitate his lifestyle, a wandering, charismatic figure. We don't have any parallels to this.

That brings us back to the archaeology of Galilee, to try to understand why such a movement happened at that particular juncture of Jewish history and the role that the social and cultural context might have played. It's a historical fact that in the first century this group emerged in Galilee. We don't know of any other movement in Galilee like it. We know of certain prophetic movements in Judea, but not within

ERICH LESSING

Galilean Judaism of the same period. So the question, as a historian, would be: What were the circumstances in Galilee that provide a context to this? And can the historian say anything about that? There archaeology can help us greatly.

Recently archaeologists have been discussing the social conditions in Galilee. Some say Galilee was impoverished by the Herodians, and Jesus is standing up for the peasants against the new ruling class. Other scholars say Galilee wasn't like that at all, and that Antipas's reign brought prosperity to the peasants; there was much intervillage trading and a lot of commercial activity. Villages like Cana, Yotapata, Bethsaida and Capernaum weren't on the decline; they were prosperous villages. So if Galilee was doing well, why would the Jesus movement emerge just then? Where is Jesus coming from? How is he going to fit into this context? Are

TAKING LIBERTIES WITH THE NATIVITY? Compared to the gospel stories of Jesus' adult public ministry, the two gospel accounts of his birth contain significant variations. Whereas Matthew 2:13–15 tells of Joseph, Mary and Jesus' flight to Egypt to escape Herod's murderous rampage (depicted above in Rembrandt's 1627 oil painting *Flight into Egypt*), the story is completely absent from Luke's gospel. Yet Matthew seems to know nothing of Mary's visit to her pregnant cousin Elizabeth, which Luke records in 1:39–56 and Raphael captured in his 16th-century painting *Visitation* (right). Although there may be some elements of historical reality in these birth narratives, Freyne sees them as the gospel writers' attempts to fill in the gaps in Jesus' life "by providing a theological introduction in story form."

there any niches, if you like, that we as historians might fit him into?

All this is reconstruction of course. But it is clear from the material remains that you had different economic and social strata in these

SCALA/ART RESOURCE, NY

Matthew and Mark, written after 70 C.E. [when the Romans destroyed the Temple at Jerusalem].

Let me go back to something you referred to earlier about the birth narratives. It sounded to me as if you had reached a negative conclusion as to their historicity.
Well, yes and no! Luke [1–2] and Matthew [1–2], the only Gospels with birth narratives, are so different in the ways they tell the story. Maybe the fact that they are so different, and yet agree on some elements of the story, might give the historian pause, to say, "Wait a minute, hold on. There is some historical reality here!" I think that may well be the case.

But I think you have to recognize that once you get into the public ministry of Jesus, that is, from John's baptism of Jesus to the Passion, the gospel writers do not deal quite as freely with the traditions about Jesus as they do in the birth narratives. The birth narratives were trying to fill in the gaps in the narrative by providing a theological introduction in story form. Matthew has the flight to Egypt; Luke knows nothing about that. Luke has the whole story of Mary going down to Elizabeth and visiting her; Matthew doesn't.

The two accounts are so very different, it seems to me that we have to be very careful in trying to collapse them into one and claim we know the details of that part of Jesus' life.

Was Jesus born in Bethlehem?
My sense would be no. He was born in Nazareth, I believe. He's never called "Jesus of Bethlehem"; he is called "Jesus of Nazareth."

Now, that said, what I would want to add is that he comes from parents who may well have roots in Bethlehem. From the second century B.C. onward, we know that *émigrés* from Judea settled in Galilee. And therefore there are strong links between Galilean Judaism and Jerusalem. There's a lot of archaeological

villages: Some people are doing better, and others are suffering as a result. The Jesus movement, it seems to me, is addressing the wealthy as well as the poor, and saying that the blessings of Israel are for all Israel. That is the inclusive vision that is at the heart of the Jesus movement. And its message was not very acceptable to those who were better off. "Woe to you, Chorazin, woe to you Bethsaida, woe to you Capernaum" [Matthew 11:21,23; Luke 10:13,15]. These villages in Galilee that we associate with

the Jesus movement are condemned because they didn't follow his message, it would seem. It is no coincidence that they are all located close to the lake and bordering the Plain of Ginnosar, whose fertility the Jewish historian Josephus praises highly, suggesting their prosperity. The rejection suggested in the woes addressed to these villages suggests that the Jesus movement gradually moves out of the region of lower Galilee and begins to move up toward Syria, as we can discern from the Gospels of

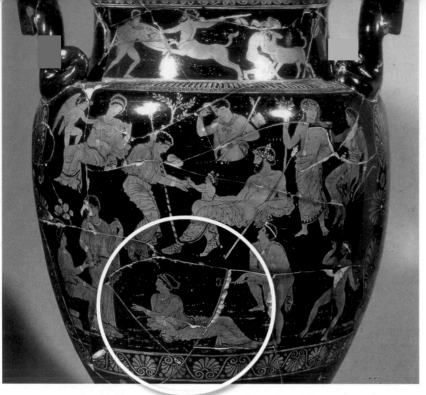

MUSEO NAZIONALE ARCHEOLOGICO DI TARANTO, TARANTO, ITALY

THE SON OF A GOD. Although there are no exact parallels for the story of the virgin birth of Jesus, other well-known tales of gods bearing children by mortals were common in the Greco-Roman world. One example is the mythical birth of Dionysus, the Greek god of wine. Zeus impregnated the princess Semele, but through the meddling of his jealous wife, Hera, Zeus revealed himself to Semele in all his divine glory, something no mortal could survive. As Semele lay dead, Zeus rescued the fetus from her womb and sewed him into his thigh. A few months later, the fully developed baby Dionysus was born from Zeus's leg, as shown on this Greek red-figure *krater* from the early fourth century B.C.E. Freyne believes that this and other similar myths of semi-divine beings made the gospel story of the virgin birth easier to accept for a Hellenistic audience.

evidence that points to continuity between Galilean and Jerusalem practices. So I would say Jesus' family may well be a Judean family who moved to Galilee. Therefore one can't dismiss entirely the possibility of links with Bethlehem [just 5 mi south of Jerusalem]. Of course, for the Christian evangelist later, the links to Bethlehem are particularly important because King David was from Bethlehem. And Jesus is called a son [a scion] of David [Matthew 1:6; Luke 1:27]. For the early Christians, that was clearly a part of the reason to say he is the Messiah. The Messiah was to come from the house of David; he's the son of David, and he, like David, was born in Bethlehem. Jesus is made to fill all the categories. But Nazareth is the more likely place in purely historical terms.

I think your question is a good one because it points to the problem we have of trying to distinguish between what is theological reflection and its development, on the one hand, and historical realities, on the other. Instead of splitting them apart and saying that's theology and that's history, I think the Bible as a whole gives us theologically interpreted history. It's the same with the origins-of-Israel question that we talked about earlier. There is an ongoing kind of reflection on historical events and rethinking them and reframing them and reinterpreting them, constantly reworking Biblical tradition itself in the process. That's why it's so hard to pull out the historical Jesus or the historical Israel and say there they are.

Where Jesus was born doesn't really affect theology, but the virgin birth comes closer ...
It does.

And resurrection is really right there.
At the heart of it.

What are the "historical Jesus" views of these?
Do you want me to have a go at answering this? Okay! Okay! People will tell me that as a historian I can't touch these questions. But I like to think that I'm a theologian as well, so I'm going to make an effort.

I think the virgin birth is the easier of the two because, although we don't quite have parallels, we do have some stories very like it. The idea of the birth of a hero like Heracles and Dionysus and the various myths of the newer gods within the Greek pantheon—the newer gods as distinct from the old Zeus and the nature gods. You have this idea of the mingling of the mortal and the immortal going on. So I think there's a tradition there in Hellenistic religious history where the story of the virgin birth would fit in very well, once people sought to attribute divine status to Jesus.

As to the Resurrection story: The tradition is very early. In 1 Corinthians [15:3–8] Paul, writing before 50 A.D., says "I handed on to you what I received," that is, a very early tradition had been established. Paul then recounts Jesus' post-Resurrection appearances. But Paul's account doesn't match the stories in the Gospels, where we have the empty tomb stories as well as the appearances to women and men [Matthew 28; Mark 16; Luke 24; John 20–21]. Eventually, the two types of stories get combined into a single narrative. You have to trace the traditions back and see—can you separate out the lines of these developments?

Now what lies behind them is something that no historian can verify. That's for sure. We are dealing with a religious claim that somehow God has approved of this man's life, approved of him in such a way that the language of "resurrection from the dead," as this was understood in

"THEY GAVE HIM A PIECE of a broiled fish and he ... ate in their presence." the supper after jesus' appearance at Emmaus recounted in Luke 24:36–42 (and shown here in a 17th-century Italian painting, *The Supper at Emmaus,* located in Florida's Ringling Museum) was meant to prove that Jesus had risen bodily from the grave. According to Freyne, Jesus' early followers believed that Jesus had triumphed over death and that God had rewarded him with a form of immortality. Although the Jewish idea of resurrection was a complex one, Freyne does not see Jesus' experience as "the resuscitation of a corpse." He believes that the supper after his Emmaus appearance reflects narrative developments and embellishments of the Resurrection story as the early Christian community came to grips with a wondrous, supernatural experience.

COLLECTION OF THE JOHN AND MABLE RINGLING MUSEUM OF ART, THE STATE ART MUSEUM OF FLORIDA, A DIVISION OF FLORIDA STATE UNIVERSITY

Jewish circles then, was deemed to be entirely appropriate. The Book of Daniel (12:2–3) envisions that the *maskilim* [12:3], the pious [or wise] ones who have been persecuted, will shine like the stars forever. Within a Jewish framework, we see the ultimate triumph of goodness, and this can be affirmed of one man in the expectation that all the just would share in this victory.

That would be the background against which I would see the development of the post-Resurrection stories. There's an experience or claim that certainly can't be verified historically, in which somehow or other the belief arose that God has approved in this way of this man Jesus. What can be established historically is the transformative effect of the claim on Jesus' first followers.

If you look at Paul—and Paul is a Jewish figure, however much he may be seen to be on the margins of Judaism for later Christian readers—Paul cannot conceive of the resurrection of one individual without the resurrection of the whole group. Read 1 Corinthians 15, and you see that

Paul is doing his damnedest to try to get at the notion of the whole people about to share in the resurrection experience. And he uses the examples of the seed, the stars, whatever. He's struggling, struggling, struggling. In the end he says, I will tell you a *mysterion*, that is, a hidden message of the divine plan for humankind. On the one hand, he shows his Jewishness that there isn't a resurrection of an individual but of a group. But secondly, that the manner of this triumph has ultimately to be left in the hands of God.

So I think that theologically we shouldn't shy away from these issues. And historically we shouldn't just dismiss them all as later developments that appear totally irrational to the modern mind. I think we can see them within the context of different forms of renewal Judaism at a very early stage, where apocalyptic hopes and wisdom traditions are intermingling and developing. The hopes associated with these expressions are all brought to bear on understanding the figure of Jesus, his life and death.

Do you envisage a physical resurrection?
No, absolutely not. Resurrection from the dead should not be confused with resuscitation of a corpse, even when some of the appearance stories give that impression as part of their narrative realism.

What do you do with the story after the resurrected Jesus returns from Emmaus [Luke 24:36–42]? And they give Jesus some broiled fish to eat to demonstrate that he's physically resurrected, not just an apparition or a spirit. What do you do with that?
There's no question about it, as stories develop—I could tell you some really good stories in Irish folklore about filling out the details of some wondrous deed or some experience that's deemed to be supernatural or preternatural. It's been vividly told, with all the details. You have to allow an oral culture to develop stories in that way. They don't create any problem for me. What we have is a tradition trying to develop that sense of the reality, the identity, that the earthly Jesus whom they knew had triumphed over death.

Thank you very much, Sean. 🖉

AUTHORS

MARK A. CHANCEY
is an Associate Professor of Religious Studies at Southern Methodist University in Dallas, Texas. His research focuses on the Historical Jesus, early Judaism, archaeology and the Bible and the political and social history of Palestine during the Roman period. Chancey is recipient of the Godbey Lecture Series Authors' Award and the Altshuler Distinguished Teaching Professor Award.

KEN DARK
received his Ph.D. in archaeology and history from the University of Cambridge. Having taught at Cambridge, Oxford and Reading, he currently serves as director of the Research Centre for Late Antiquity and Byzantine Studies at the University of Reading. Dark has excavated in Nazareth, Istanbul and various sites in Britain.

SIMON GATHERCOLE
is a Reader in New Testament studies and a Fellow at Fitzwiliam College at the University of Cambridge. He specializes in the interpretation of the New Testament and the connections between the New Testament and contemporaneous literature. Gathercole is editor of Early Christianity and author of *Defending Substitution: An Essay on Atonement in Paul* (Baker Academic, 2015).

HELMUT KOESTER
(d. 2016) was the John H. Morison Research Professor of Divinity and Winn Research Professor of Ecclesiastical History at Harvard Divinity School, where he had taught since 1958. His research was primarily in the areas of New Testament interpretation, history of early Christianity and archaeology of the early Christian period. Koester was a fellow of the American Academy of Arts a Sciences, former editor of *Harvard Theological Review* from 1975-1999 and former President of the Society of Biblical Literature.

JODI MAGNESS
is the Kenan Distinguished Professor for Teaching Excellence in Early Judaism at the University of North Carolina at Chapel Hill. Her research interests include Jerusalem, Qumran and the Dead Sea Scrolls, ancient synagogues, Masada, the Roman army in the East, and ancient pottery. Magness is currently the Director of the Huqoq Excavation Project and has excavated at a number of sites throughout Israel including Masada, Yotvata, Khirbet Yattir and Kfar Hananya.

STEVE MASON
is a Distinguished Professor of Ancient Mediterranean Religions and Cultures at the University of Groningen, Netherlands. Mason specializes in the history and literatures of the eastern Mediterranean under Roman rule, specifically Roman Judea and the Jewish historian Flavius Josephus. Mason has taught at Pennsylvania State University, York University and the University of Aberdeen and was the first Dirk Smilde Fellow at the University of Groningen in 2014. He is editor-in-chief of the first commentary series on Josephus in English (Leiden: Brill).

JEROME MURPHY-O'CONNOR
(d. 2013) was a Dominican Priest and a Professor of New Testament at the École Biblique et Archéologique in Jerusalem. Murphy-O'Connor was an authority on the Apostle Paul and received honorary degrees from Institutions in the US and abroad including a Doctorate of Literature from the National University of Ireland in University College Cork. He is the author of many books including the widely praised *The Holy Land: An Oxford Archaeological Guide from Earliest Times to 1700* (Oxford, 1998).

HERSHEL SHANKS
is the Editor of *Biblical Archaeology Review* and the founder of the Biblical Archaeology Society. He is a retired lawyer who still maintains his membership in the other bar.